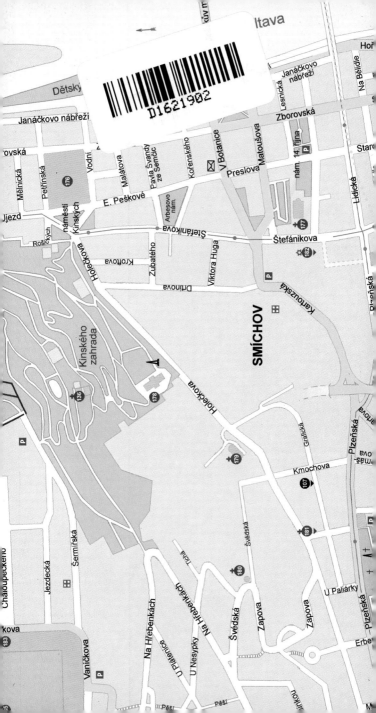

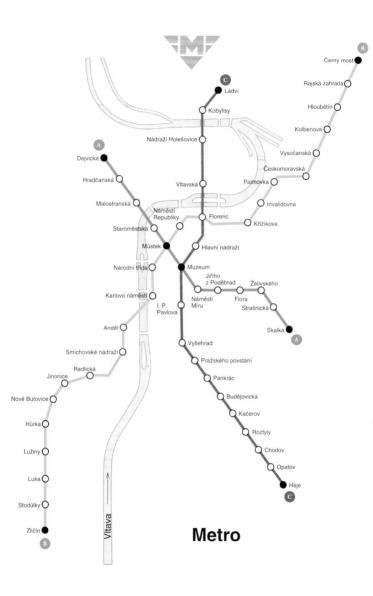

Metro

Prague

A Guide to the Golden City

by Harald Salfellner

Vitalis

The author,
Harald Salfellner,

born 1962, studied medicine in Graz and Prague and lives in the Czech capital since 1989 as editor, publisher and author. He has published a series of essays and articles as well as books about Prague, some of which have been translated into various languages (*Franz Kafka and Prague, The Golden Lane, Mozart and Prague, Das Palais Lobkowicz, Prague under water, Prague Cafés,* to name a few).

Contents

In order to exhaustively present all the beauty of and all the sights worth seeing in Prague, a much more comprehensive publication would be required than this little companion meant for a visit. Hence the book in hand contains only a selection in order to stimulate further study. Vitalis Publishers offer an extensive collection of Prague literature that assists in gaining a more profound understanding of the Golden City Prague.

The photographic material not prepared by the author himself is derived from the publisher's archive of photographic illustrations and historical publications.

1st June 2006

© Vitalis, 2006
Translated from the German original by Monica Sperling
4th edition
Printed by Finidr, Český Těšín

Brief National History

4th century BC
The Celtic Boier settle in Bohemia.

3rd century–7th century AD
Settlement of Germanic and Slavic tribes in the country.

7th century AD
Foundation of a tribal association by Franconian trader Samo.

9th century AD
Era of the Great Moravian Empire; the Czech clans come under the leadership of the Přemyslid dynasty.
Legendary age of the prophetess Libuše.
Historical era of Bořivoj I, the first Czech Prince (with his wife Ludmila) to be baptized. The royal seat is transferred to the Prague Castle [Pražský hrad].

10th century AD
Prague comes under the bishopric of Regensburg and becomes a significant trading city. Prince Wenceslas [Václav] (the saint) rules under German fiefdom until his assassination (935) through his brother Boleslav I.
In 973 AD Prague is elevated to a bishopric under the archbishopric of Mainz.
993 AD: Establishment of the existing Benedictine monastery Břevnov by Bishop Adalbert [Vojtěch].

1085 AD
Vratislav I (as King Vratislav I) is the first Bohemian Duke to receive kingship from Emperor Henry IV.

1212 AD
King Frederick II bestows on Přemysl Otakar II the privilege of a hereditary kingship ("Sicilian Golden Bull").

1278 AD
King Přemysl Otakar II during whose regime Bohemia developed into a powerful kingdom is defeated by Rudolph I of Habsburg in the battle on the Marchfeld.

1306 AD
With the assassination of Wenceslas III in Olomouc, the Přemyslid dynasty perishes owing to the lack of a male heir.

1310–1437 AD
The Luxembourgs take over the Bohemian throne.

1344 AD
Prague is elevated to an archbishopric.

1346 AD
Charles IV of Luxembourg becomes king and later Emperor of the Holy Roman Empire in 1355 AD. During his reign the late medieval city undergoes an extraordinary prime.

View of Prague by Schedel's world chronicle (1493).

1348 AD
Foundation of the first university north of the Alps and east of the Rhine.

1356 AD
The Golden Bull determines the election of the Emperor.

1378 AD
Wenceslas IV succeeds the deceased Charles IV. A period of conflicts and social, to be precise, national unrests between the Germans and the Czechs begins. John of Nepomuk is thrown into the Vltava in 1393.

1409 AD
As a consequence of the Kuttenberg decree, several students and professors leave the Charles University of Prague.

1415 AD
Reformer Jan Hus is burned at the stake in Constance.

1419 AD
First Defenestration of Prague (from the New Town City Hall). Beginning of the Hussite wars with a not only religious but also social and national character.

Jan Hus' burning at the stake in Constance.

1420 AD
The radical Hussites led by Jan Žižka triumph over Emperor Sigismund at Vítkov Hill near Prague.

1434 AD
In the battle of Lipany, the moderate Hussites defeat the radical Taborite People's Army.

1458–1471 AD
Era of the elected King George of Poděbrady [Jiří z Poděbrad].

1471–1526 AD
Period of the Polish-Lithuanian Jagiellonian dynasty. King Louis II the last Jagiellonian scion loses his life in the Turkish battle at Mohács. Bohemia (and Hungary) fall to the Habsburg family.

1526–1564 AD
Reign of Ferdinand I of Habsburg. During his regency the Jesuits are summoned to Prague.

Execution of the Bohemian gentlemen in front of the Old Town City Hall.

1526–1612 AD
Regency of Emperor Rudolph II of Habsburg; Prague becomes capital of the Holy Roman Empire and the centre of arts and sciences once again.

1618 AD
Second Defenestration of Prague marks the beginning of the Thirty Years' War.

1620 AD
The Protestant Bohemian estates are defeated by the Catholic league at the Battle of the White Mountain. The consequences are a thoroughgoing Counter-Reformation, expropriation and banishment of the old established aristocracy.

1621 AD
Ringleaders of the insurgent estates – Germans and Czechs – are executed at the Old Town Square.

Emperor Rudolph II of Habsburg.

9

In the court of Rudolph II: court jesters, scholars, artists.

1634 AD
General Albrecht of Waldstein is murdered in Cheb.

1648 AD
Swedish troops occupy the Lesser Town and Prague Castle. The Thirty Years' War ends with the Peace of Westphalia.

1721 AD
Canonization of the Bohemian martyr John of Nepomuk.

1740–1780 AD
Reign of Empress Maria Theresa; in the course of the war of succession Prague is besieged several times.

1780–1791 AD
Reign of the reformist Emperor Joseph II, innovational changes in social, political and religious fields, dissolution of numerous monasteries.

1784 AD
Union of the four towns of Prague with more than 70,000 inhabitants.

1787 AD
Mozart's first visit to Prague; premiere of his opera *Don Giovanni* at the Estates Theatre.

1792–1835 AD
Reign of Emperor Francis II; Napoleon's troops in Prague, suppression of democratic freedom endeavours by Metternich during the Restoration period.

1845 AD
Inauguration of the railway line Vienna–Prague, trade and industry flourish as a result.

W. A. Mozart (by Barbara Krafft).

Emperor Francis Joseph I.

First president of Czechoslovakia:
T. G. Masaryk.

1848 AD
Civil Revolution, Slavic Congress led by František Palacký.
The accession of Emperor Francis Joseph I whose ascension to the throne determines the fate of monarchy until his demise in 1916.

1861 AD
German majority faces defeat in the city council of Prague.

1866 AD
On the battlefield of Königgrätz, Germany's predominance over their rival Austria is guaranteed.

1882 AD
Charles University is divided into a German and a Czech university.

1891 AD
In the course of the Jubilee National Exhibition, Bohemia presents itself as a highly developed industrial state.

1897 AD
Severe anti-German violence in the streets of Prague.

1918 AD
End of the First World War, founding of the republic, Tomáš Garrigue Masaryk becomes the first president.

1920 AD
The constitution of Czechoslovakia comes into effect. Prague is transformed into a modern capital.

1938 AD
Munich Agreement: annexation of the German populated Sudetenland to the German Reich.

NS-troops march over
the Charles Bridge.

1939 AD
German units march into so-called remaining Czech country ("Resttschechei"). Establishment of the Reich Protectorate Bohemia-Moravia under German supremacy.

1942 AD
The assassination of the deputy Reich Protector Reinhard Heydrich by soldiers of the Czechoslovakian foreign army in exile triggers off the so-called "Heydrichiad" with brutal acts of retribution by the occupational authority.

The Second World War causes damage in Prague too.

1945 AD
The Prague rebellion between the 5th and the 9th of May seals the end of the "Protectorate" era and claims a large number of victims.

1945–1946 AD
On the basis of the so-called "Beneš Decrees", about three million citizens of German origin are expelled from Czechoslovakia, a large number of Sudeten Germans lose their lives to the circumstances.

Workers militia march for the communist takeover.

1948 AD
Communists' coup d'etat in Czechoslovakia, Klement Gottwald becomes president of the so-called "People's Republic" (ČSR).

1960 AD
The ČSSR constitution is passed.

1968 AD
The communist reformer Alexandr Dubček and the reform movement "Prague Spring" succumb to the tanks of the Warsaw Pact.

1969 AD
Student Jan Palach dies by self-immolation at Wenceslas Square as a protest against the oppression of his people.

Prague Spring – tanks in Prague again.

1974 AD
The first underground train (metro) is set in operation in Prague.

1977 AD
The civil rights movement Charta 77 establishes itself as the oppositional power.

1989 AD
Thousands of the GDR citizens seek refuge in the FRG Embassy in Prague and thus get permission to leave their country to go to the West. The "Velvet Revolution" brings about the end of the communist regime; the dramatist Václav Havel is elected president.

1993 AD
Following the disintegration of Czechoslovakia, the Czech and the Slovak Republics emerge as independent nations.

The dissident and president Václav Havel.

1999 AD
The Czech Republic joins NATO.

2002 AD
A flood disaster devastates large parts of the country and the inner city of Prague.

2003 AD
Václav Klaus becomes president of the Czech Republic.

2004 AD
The Czech Republic becomes a member of the European Union.

Flight of GDR citizens over the FRG Embassy fence.

The City on the Vltava

The Prague cityscape is shaped considerably by the Vltava: Altogether 17 bridges stretch over the river, the oldest and best known of them is the Charles Bridge. (In the foreground, the government building directly at the riverside not far from the Mánes Bridge).

Thanks to Smetana's symphonic poetry, the Vltava is perhaps one of the best known rivers in the world, although by world standard it is more a humble rivulet: the 31 km flowing through Prague have an average depth of about 4 m. Nonetheless, it is sufficient to ply all kinds of vehicles on: excursion ships cruise past the world famous sights, chug towards Roztoky or to the Prague Zoo and reach the Slapy Dam, the last large weir of the Vltava before Prague, in a span of only four hours from the City Centre. Humble though this rivulet might be, the Prague Steamship Company [Pražská paroplavební společnost] makes a livelihood plying its trade under 17 Prague bridges. The company's oldest and largest ship, the saloon paddle-steamer Vyšehrad with its length of 62 m, ploughed through the Vltava waves even before the Second World War. The first Bohemian

paddle-steamer is, of course, not in use anymore: the 38 m long "Bohemia" with a capacity of 140 passengers, designed by the industrialist Vojtěch Lanna and built by the Prague Engineering Works Karlín, was launched on 1ˢᵗ May 1841. The first cruise undertaken by this 32 horsepower ship, a technical masterpiece at the time, was downstream to the beautiful wine town Mělník where the Vltava eventually flows into the Elbe River and further on merges into the ocean along with it. Concerning the ocean: even the Czech Navigation Company [Česká námořní plavba] with about 20 overseas ships is based in Prague, despite the fact that its fleet that crosses the Seven Seas, cannot sail into its home port Prague.

To a proper waterway belong islands, and one can count eight within the city of Prague, apart from the peninsula Kampa. One of these islands is Marksman's Island [Střelecký ostrov] that served as training grounds for archers in the Middle Ages. A ceremonial laying of a wreath takes place on Children's Island [Dětský ostrov] on

The steamship Vyšehrad of the Prague Steam Navigation Company moored at Rašínovo nábřeží (extreme left: the Dancing House).

Motorboat Šumava under the Mánes Bridge.

the Smíchov embankment every year. On this spot is the allegorical statue of the River Vltava with the four maidens symbolising the confluence with the four rivers Berounka, Sázava, Lužnice and Otava that commemorate those drowned in the river.

The Vltava as a leisure paradise: pedalos waiting for their captains.

In the 18th century, alluvium formed the Sophie's Island [Žofín], also known as Slavic

Island, on the same level as the National Theatre. Who could have imagined that the first steam engine in Prague would puff and hiss on this river island; namely, in 1841, on a 150 m round route on tracks made of wood. Today, just as in those days, the Slavic Island is a venue for cultural events, balls, meetings, etc. Tourists can rent rowboats here and gain some experience as captains on the Vltava.

Chaser's Island [Štvanice] with a winter sport stadium on it now, is older. It owes its name to the animal chases organized here in former times.

Anybody wanting to enjoy the port atmosphere, ought to stroll below the embankment to the jetty once and admire the colourful activity and port life that has developed there; restaurant ships and so-called botels (hotels on ships) are anchored here, small cafés on the riverbanks beckon, travel agents on the lookout for clients, freshwater sailors and tourist guides wait for the next excursion ship to dock. Here too, we are welcomed by the lovely greeting "Ahoj!" again and again – there is no doubt anymore: Bohemia lies near the sea.

A restaurant-ship at Dvořák-quay prepares for the evening guests.

Prague under water

Charles Bridge: threatened by the floods.

On 12th August 2002, an unexpected tidal wave reaches the city of Prague. Karlín, Libeň, the Lesser Town – within a few hours, entire areas are engulfed in the murky floods, people and animals succumb to the flood, irreplaceable valuables and cultural possessions are destroyed. Prague residents – and with them, millions of people all over the world – wait with bated breath; Prague is under water. Tens of thousands of people are evacuated during the flood, thousands of flood helpers – police, soldiers and civilians – are brought into operation. Historic buildings are endangered, the first buildings collapse.

One of the most drastically affected institutions is the Prague Zoo, which is completely cut off from the rest. The animals are evacuated but not all can be brought to safety. A hippopotamus, a bear, a lion and the bull elephant Kadir have to be killed. The European media

Even Franz Kafka can hardly keep his head above water.

reports for several days the fate of the seal Gaston, who escapes through the Vltava into the Elbe River and all the way to Saxony to swim into a German veterinary surgeon's net near Lutherstadt Wittenberg. But alas, it doesn't end happily. Gaston dies due to exhaustion and stress on the return journey to Prague.

The flooded metro stations prove to be particularly problematic. Public transportation covering long distances come to a standstill and remains severely impeded for months. The few trams still functioning are crammed full and cannot really compensate for the cancelled underground trains.

▲ The extent of the damage done is evident only after the water ebbs. ▼

Apart from the tremendous material damage in the entire country, estimated at about 100 billion crowns, there is irreplaceable damage to the cultural heritage in the City Centre; the National Theatre, Rudolfinum, the Jewish Museum, several theatres and also private cultural institutions report severe damages. Thus, more than half a million valuable books and innumerable papers and documents from the archives are irretrievably lost.

It takes almost a week until the water ebbs away and the clearing up can progresses, but the affected areas of the city bear a ghostly resemblance for months to come.

A look at the worst affected Lesser Town. ▼

Parks and Gardens in Prague

Sea of flowers in the Vojan Garden [Vojanovy sady] in the Lesser Town.

The garden and park complexes in Prague is a world in itself! To begin with, there are the ornamental gardens of the various aristocratic palaces; the Waldstein and the Černín Garden, the Kolowrat Palace Gardens, Fürstenberg, Ledebour, Vrtba, Pállfy, Thun-Hohenstein and not to forget, the historically significant Lobkovicz Palace Garden. Some of these gardens are not accessible to the public or only on specific occasions. The Royal Gardens behind and below the Prague Castle vary in that aspect. Kafka liked to go for walks in the Chotek Gardens [Chotkovy sady] behind the Palace "Belvedere". Friends of literature marvel at the monument erected there in honour of the Czech poet Julius Zeyer. The paradise for joggers and skateboarders is only a stone's throw from here – the **Letná Park** with its manifold offer for recreational activities ranging from a children's playground to a beer-garden, attracts young and old alike in its shady tree-lined avenues in summer.

Further away from the city centre, on the Plzeňská Street, one comes across **Cibulka,** an English park. Its creator, Bishop Leopold Thun-Hohenstein from Passau, had artificial ruins built and also a Chinese pavilion, an alpine cottage, a neo-Gothic forester's house and a hermitage along with (mechanical) hermits. A stream, a waterfall and a grotto had to be included too.

Funicular at the Petřín Hill.

The **Klamovka**, also situated on the Plzeňská Street, is a former rural farm within a surrounding park complex. The name comes from the noble family Clam-Gallas. Here too, the neo-Gothic gallery, a rococo chapel and a pavilion remind one of better times, but the little park with a simple restaurant with a public garden is still a popular destination for the residents of the surrounding area.

Further on towards the outskirts is the **Břevnov Monastery** with its historical public garden from the 18th century and the little castle Vojtěška and a miraculous spring. A tram ride further away from town and one comes to the **Game Preserve Hvězda** [obora Hvězda] with a star-shaped Renaissance palace built by Emperor Ferdinand I. In 1797 the woods underwent its transformation into a leisure park with walkways and benches.

A look at the Royal Gardens behind Prague Castle.

In the Orchard Stromovka]. ▼

An outing worth undertaking is to a park complex accessible from the Lesser Town, namely to **Petřín Hill** with its peaceful corners and footways, its rose gardens, old trees and flower beds, and also with monuments, objects of interest and diversions. In summer, a funicular leads from the Lesser Town up to the iron observation tower.

The **Royal Enclosure** [Královská obora] also known as the **Orchard** [Stromovka], with an expanse of over a million square metres, is the metropole's largest park. Originally in the ownership of Bohemian kings, a game enclosure

Walk in the Royal Gardens; St Vitus Cathedral in the background.

was maintained here during the rule of Přemysl Otakar II. One actually came across camels here! In past centuries, the orchard was connected to the Prague Castle by a chestnut tree avenue, but the avenue was deforested during the French Wars. Since its transformation into a park complex in 1850, the orchard is a popular excursion spot among Prague residents. The Prague Exhibition Grounds are also situated here with the frequently visited panorama picture of the Hussite Battle of Lipany (1434) that is extremely important in the national history.

Pavilion in the gardens on the southern castle slope.

The Prague Zoo and the magnificent Baroque Chateau Troja are only a short distance from here. On a slope shines Vladislav Jagiello's **Governor's summer palace**; it was rebuilt in a neo-Gothic style in the 19th century and houses the Prague National Museum's library and reading room. The remains of the

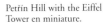

Petřín Hill with the Eiffel Tower en miniature.

so-called **Imperial Mill**, a cutting mill used for working on glass and precious stones, can be found beneath the palace. The palace was gifted to Emperor Rudolph II by the corporative states and was, later on in the 19th century, one of old Austria's most important paper factories. A more than 100 m long tunnel was dug through the Letná-massif in those days, the so-called **Rudolph Tunnel**, in order to divert the Vltava water to a large pond in the Royal Enclosure. Remains of the technical structures can still be seen.

At Prague Cemeteries

Amongst the dozens of cemeteries in Prague a few are interesting even for strangers. No doubt the most important of these quiet but much visited churchyards is **Vyšehrad**, the Czech National Graveyard where several great personalities of the Czech nation have been laid to rest; Poets like Jan Neruda, Karel Čapek, Karel Hynek Mácha and Jaroslav Vrchlický, painters like Max Švabinský, Alfons Mucha or Mikoláš Aleš, composers like Antonín Dvořák, Zdeněk Fibich or Bedřich Smetana.

Probably the most visited graveyard however is not Vyšehrad but the **Old Jewish Cemetery** in the Jewish Quarter of Prague. The **New Jewish Cemetery** in Prague Strašnice also attracts many visitors because here indeed is the the most renowned grave in this city, Franz Kafka's last resting place. The extended complex of the Olšany Cemetery [Olšanské hřbitovy] borders on the New Jewish Cemetery. Here, at the **Olšany Cemetery,** one of the largest cemeteries in Europe, lies a distinguished row of significant personalities from the 19th century, for example, the artists August Piepenhagen, Luděk Marold, Josef Lada and Josef Mánes, the philosopher Bernard Bolzano and the poet Karel Jaromír Erben. More than a million people have been buried at Olšany, about 100,000 graves are lined up on the round 42 km of passageways. Entirely different from the frequently visited Olšany is the long abandoned **Lesser Town Cemetery**, a kingdom fallen into a fairy-tale sleep in the midst of thundering traffic. The couple Dušek who so hospitably recieved Wolfgang Amadeus Mozart in Prague and Vincenz Morstadt, the creator of several Prague views, also rest here. A large graveyard complex can also be found in **Vinohrady**. Quite a few known personalities from recent Czech cultural history are buried here, for example, Václav Havel the builder of the Lucerna Palace and grandfather of the subsequent president, or even Jan Karafiát the author of the well known Czech children's book *Broučci* (*Fireflies*). The burial place of the author Jakub Arbes is in the churchyard **Malvazinky** in Smíchov. Somewhat on the outskirts, we come across the philosopher Jan Patočka's grave at the **Březnov Graveyard**. Even the benefactor Johann August Klaar, from Úštěk (Auscha) in North Bohemia, founder of the first Institution for the Blind in Prague, is also buried here.

Prague House Symbols

Long before the people of Prague characterised their houses with numbers, they differentiated their buildings from each other by the so-called house symbols. The house symbols mostly have a connection, though often not relevant today, with the history of the house or the trade practiced (bells, cans, rings, goblets, keys, etc.). The house symbols (animals, especially lions and lambs, donkeys and bears, carp and snakes, furthermore candles, shoes, violins, wheels, hearts, angels, stars, grapes, horseshoes and many more) were created in a variety of colours and were depicted in stucco, chiselled in stone, painted on the façade or forged in iron and bestowed on the buildings melodious names like "At the Blue Snake" or "At the Golden Swan".

The craftsmanship and the artistic dexterity of the old masters are just as worthy of our admiration as the poetic skills and fantasy of the ancestral house owners. Many of these symbols are similar to each other or even exist several times in Prague because the different parts of town were independent from each other in those days. Many of these minor works of art that have been lovingly tended to can be seen especially along the Royal Path, in the Celetná Lane or in Nerudova Street in the Lesser Town.

In 1770 a consecutive chronological numbering of buildings with the so-called conscription numbers (white numbers on a red background) was ordered, the present-day orientation numbers (white script on a blue background) are common since 1878. With that, the often very charming, witty and easy-to-remember house symbols have eventually become reminiscent of the past – a pity, actually!

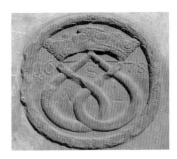

About the Architecture of the 20ᵗʰ Century

Figurehead on the Čech-Bridge (art nouveau).

The television tower in Žižkov (futurism). ▶

Villa Müller (functionalism).

On the whole, large numbers of visitors come to Prague to see an intact historical city and let the air of the past centuries sink in. But even the 20ᵗʰ century has left its mark on the face of the city – with masterly buildings and buildings of timeless design, but also with architecture which simply looks terrible.

Art nouveau dominated at the beginning of the 20ᵗʰ century, unfolding itself in harmony with the national romantic folklore. After the First World War, cubism triumphed but was displaced in the twenties by functionalism, the avant garde movement. The architecture of the Slovenian architect Josip Plečnik who had been appointed to the city on the Vltava, is worthy of a special note and he remodelled, among others, the Prague Castle in the vein of the new republic. The Second World War and the ensuing integration in the communist sphere of influence brought the developments more or less to a standstill. A circle of prefab buildings, megalomanic prestigious buildings and gigantic traffic projects resulted in sensitive losses to the cityscape. One of the largest building projects of the century was an underground train network through the seventies. With a city expressway, the "magistrála", brutally built through the city centre region, a car-friendly traffic politics was practiced – the idyllic city park and the elegant square in front of the train station were sacrificed. The collapse of the socialist regime eventually brought new possibilities and of course, great risks too. Would the incomparable cityscape suffer even more damage through the incessant investment boom? The protection

of historical monuments, as a rule, cannot exist against the astronomical sums from international investors.

The most important architectonic achievements of the 20th century can be cited in just a few examples. Bearing in mind the city centre, there are: the renovation of the **Prague Castle complex** since the twenties, the rebuilding of the **Prague central station** by Josef Fanta (1901–1909), the **Svatopluk-Čech Bridge** (1905–1908), the cubist building **"House of the Black Madonna"** by Josef Gočár (1911–1912), the art nouveau **Municipal House** adjacent to the Powder Tower by Osvald Polívka and Antonín Balšánek (1905–1912), the palace occupied by the insurance company **Riunione Adriatica di Sicurtà** on Jungmannova Street (1922–1925), the splendid buildings on Wenceslas Square – the **department store Peterka** by Jan Kotěra (1899–1900), the **Secession Grandhotel Europa** by Bendlmayer, Letzl and Hypšman (1903–1905), the **Koruna Palace** by Antonín Pfeiffer (1911–1914), the **Lindt store** (1925–1927) and the **Baťa store** (1927–1929) by Ludvík Kysela, the **Hotel Juliš** by Pavel Janák (1928–1933).

One of Prague's first reinforced concrete skeleton constructions is on the Vodičkova Street – the **Lucerna Palace** built by Vácslav Havel, grandfather of the future President Václav Havel; not very far from here is the striking art nouveau Palace **"U Nováků"** by Osvald Polívka. From the Vltava embankment of Masarykovo nábřeží greets the functionalist romantic **Mánes House** by Otakar Novotný (1927–1930). Grossly disturbing is the annexe to the National Theatre, the **Nová Scéna** made of Cuban glass components. **The Dancing House** [Tančící dům] (also called the Ginger and Fred Building) on the Vltava quay, a prestigious building designed by Frank O. Gehry is also controversial.

One comes across even more interesting examples of modern architecture on the outskirts of the city than in the city centre: the **Žižka monument** by Jan Zázvorka at Vítkov Hill (1926–1932), the **Municipal Waterworks** by Antonín Engel in Podolí (1923–1928), the **Film studios** and restaurant by Max Urban in Barrandov (1929–1934), the **Baba Villas** in Dejvice (1928–1934), **Villa Müller** by Adolf Loos in Střešovice (1928–1930), the **Prague Exhibition Palace** by Oldřich Tyl and Josef Fuchs in Holešovice (1924–1928) or the **St Wenceslas Church** by Josef Gočár in Vršovice (1928–1933).

Of Czech Beer

Czech beer has an excellent reputation all over the world. The famous "Pilsner Urquell" [Plzeňský Prazdroj] and the "Original Budweiser" are naturally tapped all over the country but even the lesser known brands can hold upright: Krušovice's dark beer, the tasty "Bernard" from the family brewery Humpolec, the "Starobrno" from the "Erste Brünner Actienbrauerei" (First Brno Joint Stock Brewery) established in 1872, or the "Regent" a brew from Třeboň, the presumably oldest brewery in this country. Not to be omitted are naturally the successors to the throne in the world famous beer cities: Not only does the Urquell come from Plzeň but also the popular ten degree "Gambrinus" and in the south Bohemian České Budějovice originates also the "Samson". Prague of course brews its own excellent beer, and this since the 11th century! Since 1871, the Prague Joint Stock Brewery in Smíchov delivers the mild ten degree "Staropramen" that has moulded itself as the absolute Prague Beer.

The competitor obviously views it differently, for example **"U Fleků"**, the legendary

and original Prague brewery restaurant where beer comfort is the winning factor. This tavern has sold the unsurpassable Flek beer since the 15th century. It was only in 1762 that a certain Jakub Flekovský took over the pub in its existing name and helped it take a step towards success. 6,000 hectolitres of the dark beer with a caramel taste produced from Prague water, hop from Žatec and four different malts is poured out annually and many beer tourists smack their lips even years later at the thought of the delicious drop in the noisy though incomparable atmosphere.

Nevertheless, "U Fleků" is not the only one worth a visit, other public places also attract with their unmistakable charm. The beer restaurant **"U Kalicha"** is well-known from Jaroslav Hašek's novel *The Good Soldier Švejk*. A visit to this pub is on the standard agenda for hearty beer drinkers.

In the Thomas Lane [Tomášská] in the Lesser Town, the **St Thomas Cellar** holds its ground since the 14th century; they even served a black beer produced in their own brewery until 1953. Adventurous beer friends are recommended an expedition to the Žižkov area on the outskirts of the city centre, well-known among night revellers – here one can still find many pubs with originality and spared by tourism.

The clock at the restaurant "U Fleků".

Pilsner Joint-Stock Brewery complex where the probably most popular beer in the world is brewed.

The *"Velvet Revolution"*

In the summer of 1989 thousands of Germans from the GDR fled to the embassy of the FRG in order to escape from the East into the West. The streets were parked full with "Trabbis" and Wartburgs. Ultimately, the German Minister for Foreign Affairs, Hans-Dietrich Genscher, announced to the persistent refugees in the provisional emergency lodgings that they had been granted permission to exit from the East. Then came the memorable day of 9th November when the Berlin Wall fell. In Czechoslovakia reigned – yet – a suspenseful quiet. On 17th November 1989 the situation escalated, the uncertain police beating up students demonstrating against the totalitarian regime. One of the last bastions of European Communism began to sway. Soon after, the demonstrating students were followed by actors and artists, academics and workers. The streets filled up, intimidated operational troops anxiously watched the swelling national movement. Hundreds of thousands of Prague residents gathered at Wenceslas Square. With bunches of keys, the

Summer 1989: GDR-citizens flee to the FRG Embassy.

crowds fir
arian Peop
ership had
hands of t
citizen's fe
positional
resigned
ber, ¾ m
field to s
forms. T
triumph,
an exube
the hour
Spring I
renowne
from the
It didn
Havel n

These turbulent days are known as the "Velvet Revolution" but one forgets that there was thrashing and cudgelling and that nobody was certain whether the uniformed would use firearms to quell the uprising. One tends to forget the fear and the anxiety and remembers only the happiness when the nightmare lasting decades finally came to an end and the future could begin.

November 1989: Václav Havel and Alexandr Dubček speak to the gently demonstrating masses at Wenceslas Square.

Defenestrations of Prague

Contemporary engraving of the Second Defenestration of Prague (1618).

It is a popular old Czech custom, mock some, to push political opponents out of a suitable window into the depths when the opportunity arises. As a matter of fact, one knows of

many such harsh treatments even in the dim and distant past. Three defenestrations, in a close sense, are particularly ingrained in the memory of the Prague folk. Firstly there is the so-called First Defenestration of Prague, where the radical Hussites threw a judge and several councillors from a window of the City Hall in the New Town of Prague. 11 human lives were lost in this ambush. Then one remembers the defenestration on 23rd May 1618 when Bohemian Protestants dispatched two imperial councillors and their secretary from the Bohemian Chancellery. The torture ended lightly for the unfortunate three – they made a soft landing, as the rumour goes, on a dung heap. But the defenestration lit the torch for the outbreak of the Thirty Years' War that destroyed the empire to a large extent and drastically decimated its population.

The Third Defenestration of Prague marked the end of Jan Masaryk, son of the republic's first president. In the year of the coup 1948, he fell out of the window of the Černín Palace to his death under unresolved circumstances. The demise of this politician is considered to be a result of a political conspiracy.

crowds finally jangled the end of the totalitarian People's Democracy; the communist leadership had no choice but to leave power in the hands of the dissidents and the opposition. A citizen's forum was established as a basis of oppositional power, the communist government resigned on 24th November, on 25th November, ¾ million Czechs gathered at the Letná field to stress their demands for political reforms. Then the general strike followed by triumph, victory – the protest passed over into an exuberant celebratory mood. The men of the hour were Alexandr Dubček, the Prague Spring hero in 1968, and Václav Havel, the renowned dramatist who had been released from the state prison only a few months earlier. It didn't take long before the walls read: Havel na Hrad – Havel to the Castle!

These turbulent days are known as the "Velvet Revolution" but one forgets that there was thrashing and cudgelling and that nobody was certain whether the uniformed would use firearms to quell the uprising. One tends to forget the fear and the anxiety and remembers only the happiness when the nightmare lasting decades finally came to an end and the future could begin.

November 1989: Václav Havel and Alexandr Dubček speak to the gently demonstrating masses at Wenceslas Square.

Defenestrations of Prague

Contemporary engraving of the Second Defenestration of Prague (1618).

It is a popular old Czech custom, mock some, to push political opponents out of a suitable window into the depths when the opportunity arises. As a matter of fact, one knows of

many such harsh treatments even in the dim and distant past. Three defenestrations, in a close sense, are particularly ingrained in the memory of the Prague folk. Firstly there is the so-called First Defenestration of Prague, where the radical Hussites threw a judge and several councillors from a window of the City Hall in the New Town of Prague. 11 human lives were lost in this ambush. Then one remembers the defenestration on 23rd May 1618 when Bohemian Protestants dispatched two imperial councillors and their secretary from the Bohemian Chancellery. The torture ended lightly for the unfortunate three – they made a soft landing, as the rumour goes, on a dung heap. But the defenestration lit the torch for the outbreak of the Thirty Years' War that destroyed the empire to a large extent and drastically decimated its population.

The Third Defenestration of Prague marked the end of Jan Masaryk, son of the republic's first president. In the year of the coup 1948, he fell out of the window of the Černín Palace to his death under unresolved circumstances. The demise of this politician is considered to be a result of a political conspiracy.

Prague Spring '68

Czechoslovakia was an orthodox socialist People's Republic on Soviet Union's side since 1948. Then in the sixties, the distinct political thaw set in. The leader of the communist party then, Alexandr Dubček, introduced reforms in 1968 nurturing hopes of a free and independent development in the country. The USSR protector could not watch this without taking action. On 21st August 1968 armed forces of the Warsaw pact marched into Czechoslovakia and ended the reform era by force. In the following years of "Normalisation", Czechoslovakia was taken in hand by the ally, the reforms were cancelled and the political leadership of the so-called Prague Spring deprived of power. As a result, a large number of intellectuals, writers and artists left the country or went into hiding. The much longed-for change took place only in 1989 with the "Velvet Revolution".

Wenceslas Square is an important scene of political manifestations.

1968: Young demonstrators protest against the marching in of the Warsaw Pact troops.

Prague and Music

Bohemian musicians.

Prague is one of the most traditional music metropolises in Europe, the Czechs one of the most important musical nations in this world since time immemorial! There is singing, music and concerts everywhere, in churches, palaces and concert halls. Antonín Dvořák, Zdeněk Fibich and Bedřich Smetana lived in Prague, Josef Mysliveček, "the divine Bohemian" (Il divino Boemo) was born here, Leoš Janáček and Bohumil Martinů celebrated their greatest successes here.

Generations of Bohemian musicians were educated at the renowned **Prague Conservatorium**; Czech masters went out into the world from here. Even foreign maestros gladly performed in Prague because they found a discerning audience enraptured by music; to name some, Antonio Vivaldi and Wolfgang Amadeus Mozart, Ludwig van Beethoven and

Billboards announcing concerts all over the city.

Carl Maria von Weber, Niccolò Paganini, Franz Liszt, Frédéric Chopin and Peter Illyich Tchaikovsky.

The traditional festival "Prague Spring" [Pražské jaro] has an excellent reputation and in the meantime, a second festival has joined in – the "Prague autumn" [Pražský podzim].

Considered amongst the most important music abodes in the city are the **National Theatre**, the **Estates Theatre**, and the **State Opera**, the former new German Theatre and moreover the **House of Artists** [Rudolfinum], the **Smetana Hall** in the Municipal House [Obecní dům], the **House at the Stone Bell** at Old Town Square and a number of churches where concerts are held. The **Villa Amerika**, the creation of the Baroque master builder Kilian Ignaz Dientzenhofer in the New Town houses an Antonín Dvořák Museum worth seeing. Not far from the Charles Bridge, in the **Smetana Museum** at the Novotný footbridge [Novotného lávka] opened in 1936, memorabilia from Bedřich Smetana's life are stored: manuscripts, photographs, fragments of his diary, correspondence, the programme of his first concert in Prague, a silver conductor's baton, whose oldest preserved composition – *The Gallop in D-Major* from 1832 – as well as the piano on which he composed the operas *Libuše* and *The Bartered Bride.*

Czech jazz virtuoso at the Charles Bridge.

Statue of Antonín Dvořák in front of the Rudolfinum.

The Czech Philharmonic, the most significant orchestra of the nation, performs in all the great concert halls across the world. Known solely on the banks of the Vltava however is the Secession "Hlahol" on the Vltava, in that it fosters native choral singing. Many tourists naturally visit the Mozart landmarks in Prague, foremost the **Villa Bertramka** in Smíchov where chamber concerts resound on warm summer evenings. Prague has a lot of to offer for jazz fans too; for example, the **Jazzclub Reduta** where even Bill Clinton in his time reached for the saxophone. On the Charles Bridge and other public places one often hears Dixieland and Swing. Even a zither-player lets his music unfold under the open sky and when one greets the modest musician one is suddenly engaged in conversation with an authority on old stringed instruments.

Mozart and Prague

Impression from Mozart's time: Gallant couple at the Fürstenberg Garden.

Besides Salzburg and Vienna, Prague is the third metropolis inseparably associated with the name Mozart. The composer celebrated his greatest triumphs in the Bohemian capital, even the singers of street ballads and street urchins understood the aria in his operas while the audience in the royal capital Vienna wrinkled their illustrious noses at them. All in all, the conductor Wolfgang Amadeus Mozart visited the capital on the Vltava five times, three of them were longer stays: in January and February 1787 for a cheerful Prague trip where he introduced himself to be impressed audience of his opera *Le nozze di Figaro* (The Wedding of

Estates Theatre in the Old Town of Prague.

Das ständ. Theater mit dem Universitäts oder Carolingebäude.
gegen Mitternacht.
Verlegt bei Franz Zimmer & Sohn in Prag.

Figaro), then in autumn 1787 when he attended the première of his opera *Don Giovanni* in the Estates Theatre, and finally in 1791 when he was instructed to compose an opera on the occasion of the coronation of Leopold II as king of Bohemia (*La clemenza di Tito*). Amongst Mozart's friends in Prague were the Czech composer František Dušek and his wife, the singer Josepha Dušková. Without doubt, the, most popular place connected with Mozart in Prague today – the Villa Bertramka, a country estate in the Smíchov district – belonged to this couple. Mozart was a guest here several times and created many of his beautiful works in this idyllic setting. His friendly sentence "My Prague folk understand me." has gone down in the annals of the history of the city.

Villa Bertramka in Smíchov.

St Nepomuk, the Bridge Guardian

In all of Bohemia, throughout Europe, actually all over the world, we encounter him as the silent guard on bridges and passageways. Whether in the wooded valleys of Carinthia in Austria, in the Tuscany villages or in the South American states – he is the guardian saint of the seal of confession and his likeness is worshipped in innumerable churches. And a part of Prague is almost always portrayed with him – the Charles Bridge made of stone. That is namely where the pious John from the Bohemian town Nepomuk had to renounce his life as a martyr in 1393 AD. King Wenceslas IV had him thrown into the tide from the stone bridge over the River Vltava. The legend goes that he did not wish to divulge the pious Queen Sophie's confessional secret as demanded by the cruel king – hence he had to forfeit his life.

His afterlife as the popular national saint began with its signs and miracles in Prague. The legend relates as follows: *"Nobody knew where the corpse lay. But the water level that was higher at the beginning of the year was conspicuously lower so that the literally drying up of the River Vltava was considered godsent. The corpse became visible. However, the king in his hatred would not permit it to be lifted. On the night of 17 to 18 April, wonderful lights shone on the corpse. Attracted by the glow, everybody came together to see the holy corpse. The canons lifted him without worrying about the king's rage and carried him into the Chapel of the Holy Cross until a meritable tomb had been prepared for the holy one in the cathedral ... In 1719 the grave was*

exhumed, the bones were in good condition and the tongue was not decomposed, only dried up. During an examination, it turned a living dark red colour and shape that intensified to a crimson colour over the span of two hours. Thus did God glorify this part of the body that after having dutifully remained silent now speaks louder and even more emphatically in all its entirety."

Almost 300 years after his martyrdom in 1683, the bronze statue of St Nepomuk made by Johann Brokoff was installed on the Charles Bridge.

The cult of St Nepomuk gravitated especially during the Baroque age and after his canonisation in 1721 towards its culminating point: the saint's magnificent silver tomb in St Vitus Cathedral originated during this time. As a result, on 16th May, the feast day of St John of Nepomuk, believers flock to Prague in order to commemorate the Holy John with prayers and devout celebrations at the Charles Bridge.

The queen confesses; scene from the Nepomuk legend at the statue on the Charles Bridge.

▼

The Golem

The Golem, so the legend goes, was an artificial being made of clay. The Prague Rabbi Loew created him according to a secret ritual in order to protect the Prague Jewry. After his awakening, he was given the name Josef and the rabbi wrapped him in the clothes of a Shammes. Though the Golem could not speak, he obediently fulfilled the tasks assigned to him with zealousness and devotion. Under certain circumstances however, the zealous and good-natured servant could turn into a dangerous monster, rage through the Jewish city like a berserker and wreak destruction.

Various portrayals of the Golem in fine arts.

Once, as the Golem raged through the Jewish Town, the esteemed Rabbi Loew transformed him into a lump of clay again in the attic of the Old-New Synagogue. In those days, the rabbi declared it as strictly forbidden to enter the attic of the synagogue ever again.

There are various differing Golem legends, and even the Golem figure is known not only to the people in Prague. But an often read novel by the Prague writer Gustav Meyrink bearing the title *The Golem* has contributed a lot to works popularising the figure and attaching it to Prague. Literary adaptations, films, creations of fine arts – in addition to a general interest in Jewish Prague and the esoteric doctrines of Judaism – made the Golem into a central figure of the Prague Jewish Quarter.

Franz Kafka and Prague

Kafka's place of work: Worker's Accident Insurance Company for the kingdom of Bohemia.

Kafka's circle of life: Old Town Square.

"... a book ought to be an axe for the frozen sea in us. That's what I believe."

Today Franz Kafka is a synonym for Prague like none other. Ironically, all his life the German Jewish writer wanted to get away from his birthplace of which he said: "Prague won't let go ... We would have to set fire to two places, Vyšehrad and the Prague Castle, and then it might be possible for us to get away."

The future lawyer Franz Kafka was born in 1883 on the outskirts of the then existing Prague ghetto. After his university education at the Prague German University, Kafka worked as an insurance lawyer in the Prague Workers Accident Insurance Institution. The poet's private life was strongly

influenced by his father who was felt to be superior and his own inability to decide on marriage. He broke off his engagement to Felice Bauer from Berlin twice; the relationship with the married Czech journalist Milena Jesenská was of great significance.

Franz Kafka's first prose volume *Meditation* was published with a small number of copies in 1912. In the following years, Kafka was considered an acknowledged author in authoritative literary circles, although he did not live to experience his success as a writer of international standard. A tuberculosis ailment resulted in Kafka's early retirement and eventually, a premature death. He died in a sanatorium in Kierling near Vienna in 1924. His friend Max Brod prevented the loss of the unpublished literary works destined to testamentary destruction and published Kafka's works posthumously.

The novels published especially after his demise are considered as the most outstanding creations of the 20th-century German literature. Kafka's works are read worldwide and have attracted a constant, almost not assessable flood of interpretations. Amongst his most important works are the novels *The Trial* and *The Castle*, the narrations *The Verdict* and *The Metamorphosis*, in addition to diaries and letters (to his sister Ottla, his fiancée Felice, his lover Milena) as well as the biographical roman-à-clef *Letter to Father*.

"Kafka was Prague and Prague was Kafka. Never was it so perfect and so typical Prague and never more ought it to be so as during Kafka's lifetime. And we, his friends, we knew that this Prague was contained everywhere in Kafka's works in the finest detail."

(Johannes Urzidil)

Kafka as a grammar school student.

Kafka at the age of 31 years.

Kafka with his fiancee Felice Bauer.

10 x Prague Literature

Bohumil Hrabal (1914–1997), born in Brno, spent his childhood in central Bohemian Nymburk and studied law in Prague. After the communist coup, Hrabal worked amongst others as a blast furnace worker in Kladno and as a scene shifter in the Prague Theatre. Since 1962 he devoted himself exclusively to the literary work whereby his own experiences provide the backdrop for his to a great extent autobiographical prose. Although he did not submit to the socialist doctrine he was caught in the cross-fire of censorship several times and could publish his works only in the so-called "Samisdat" or in exiled publishing houses. Hrabal succeeded (besides Milan Kundera and Jaroslav Seifert) in becoming one of the most important post-war authors in Czechoslovakia. Received worldwide and read by millions, his writings centred on the fate of the ordinary man and penetrated by his earthy humour could be published unmutilated in his homeland only after 1989. At that point of time, Hrabal was already a famous author respected in the literary world. After the "Velvet Revolution" the poet, living in rural seclusion, became something like the Godfather on the Olympus of Czech literature. A fall from the hospital window that he climbed out of to feed the pigeons ended, in 1997, his life spanning over almost a century.

Important works:
Dancing Lessons for the Advanced in Age (1964)
The Palaverers (1964)
Cutting it Short (1976)
Snowdrop Festivities (1980)
I Served the King of England (1982)

Franz Werfel (1890–1945) was born in Prague. The novelist, narrator and lyricist Franz Werfel was from an established Jewish factory owner's family. Even as a student of the New Town German Grammar School, Werfel composed poems and wrote dramas, in 1910 the famous expressionist lyricist was already considered the focal point of the Prague "Arco"-Circle. From 1912 he worked as a publisher's reader for the Kurt Wolff Publishers in Leipzig; for them he initiated the avant-garde series *Der Jüngste Tag* (*The Judgement Day*). After taking part in the First World War, he moved to Vienna where he married Gustav Mahler's widow. He was forced to leave Vienna in 1938 and went into exile. He arrived in the USA, with detours, and there he succumbed to a heart ailment at the end of the war. At the centre of his literary and essayist works are problems of faith as well as the battle against the disintegration of values. He achieved great success with the readers for his novels *Embezzled Heaven* (1939) and *The Song of Bernadette* (1941).

Other important works:
Verdi. A Novel of the Opera (1924)
The Forty Days of Musa Dagh (1933)
The Star of the Unborn (1946)

Jan Neruda (1834–1891), born in the Lesser Town in Prague, grew up in poor conditions. His father worked in the barracks kitchen and his mother as a housemaid. He was forced to give up a hopefully begun law and philosophy education due to financial reasons. Neruda worked as a local reporter since 1856 and with time his first poetry and prose were created. In his writings the naturalistic author expounds the fate of the Czech nation.

His significant prose writing *Arabesky* (*Arabesques*) was published in 1864, in 1878 followed the even nowadays much-read *Prague Tales from the Little Quarter* in which he immortalises, often in an ironic manner, the

destinies of the odd and ordinary people of this part of town.

Other important works:
Cemetery Flowers (1858)
Cosmic Songs (1878)
Ballads and Romances (1883)

Johannes Urzidil (1896–1970), born in Prague, studied German and Slavonic philology and art history at the Charles University. In the twenties he worked as press adviser of the German embassy in Prague and mingled with the literary circles of his homeland (among others, with Franz Werfel, Franz Kafka and Max Brod). Urzidil made a name for himself even before the Second World War not only as an expressionist lyricist but also as a cultural historian and editor. In 1939 he emigrated to England via Italy and further on to the USA in 1941. Urzidil gained literary recognition for his narrative works after the war. In 1964 he was awarded the great Austrian State Prize.

Important works:
The Fall of the Damned (1919)
Goethe in Böhmen (*Goethe in Bohemia*) (1932)
The Lost Lover (1956)
The Prague Triptych (1960)

Leo Perutz (1882–1957) was the offspring of a Jewish business family in Prague. He moved to Vienna with his family when he was 17. After training in the insurance business he was employed as an actuary for several years. His first work *The Third Bullet* (1915) brought him success, immediately followed by his next novel *From Nine to Nine* (1918). Friedrich Torberg characterises Perutz as a "moral lapse between Franz Kafka and Agatha Christie." At the beginning of the twenties, Perutz gave up his middle-class job in favour of an existence as an independent writer. The tide turned after the seizure of power by the National Socialists; his writings were banned in Germany.

Perutz was forced to leave Austria in 1938 and emigrate to Israel. His work disappeared into oblivion for a long time and experienced a renaissance in the 1990s.

Other important works:
Little Apple (1928)
The Swedish Cavalier (1936)
By Night under the Stone Bridge (1953)

Egon Erwin Kisch (1885–1948), born in Prague, came from a reputable Jewish draper family. He worked as a local reporter and acquired an intimate knowledge of Prague life. In *Aus Prager Gassen und Nächten* (*From the Lanes and Nights in Prague*), a work published in 1912, portrays above all the socially isolated environment of brothels and public houses. Similarly his only novel *Der Mädchenhirt* (*The Shepherd of Girls*) (1914) is an account of this demi-monde. After the First World War, Kisch engaged himself with the communist party and worked for the journals *Weltbühne* (*World Stage*) and *Rote Fahne* (*Red Flag*) in Berlin. Kisch attained great popularity with his volume *The Racing Reporter* (1924), a coverage of current events that brought him the homonymous nickname. Being a communist, he was forced to go into exile in 1933 that took him via France, Great Britain and Spain to Mexico. Shortly after the end of the war he returned to Prague where he died soon after.

Other important works:
The Case of Colonel Redl (1924)
Rush Through Time (1926)
Discoveries in Mexico (1945)

Gustav Meyrink (1868–1932) born in Vienna, came to Prague as a 16 year-old. The subsequently renowned novelist and narrator founded a Christian banking house but faced opposition, especially in middle-class circles due to his eccentric lifestyle. Meyrink's existence in Prague was ruined after a three-month imprisonment so he was compelled to leave the city in 1903. After intermediate stops in

Vienna and Munich he settled down in Starnberg. His novel *The Golem* (1915) that helped him to worldwide fame was created here. Meyrink is considered the founder of fantastic literature. Typical of his works are mystical influences and a tendency to occultism.

Other important works:
The Green Face (1917)
Walpurgisnacht (Walpurgis Night) (1917)
The White Dominican (1921)
The Angel of the West Windows (1927)

Jaroslav Hašek (1883–1923) was born in Prague. After studying at the commercial college and a short-term occupation as a bank employee he led the life of a vagrant and bohemian since 1902. He travelled through the entire Austria-Hungary and Europe. Hašek sympathised with the then modern anarchist movement, edited their periodicals and wrote instigatory feuilletons and humorous sketches. In order to ridicule the German parliament elections he founded the "Party of Moderate Progress within the limits of Law". At the outbreak of the First World War, he went to the Russian front and joined the Czechoslovakian legionaries taking detours in his stride. After the October Revolution he worked as a journalist for the Red Army. He returned to Prague in 1920, withdrew from politics, made his appearance in the cabaret "Červená sedma" (Red Seven) and dedicated himself to the composition of the *Good Soldier Švejk* (1912–1923) which was initially rejected by contemporary critics as vulgar and inartistic. Only after the novel was translated into German was it a big success and found entry into world literature as a significant Czech work.

Important works:
Dobrý voják Švejk a jiné podivné historky
(*The Good Soldier Švejk and other peculiar anecdotes*) (1912)
Dobrý voják Švejk v zajetí
(*The Good Soldier Švejk in captivity*) (1917)
The Fateful Adventures of the Good Soldier Švejk during the World War (1921–23)

Karel Čapek (1890–1938), son of a country doctor from Malé Svatoňovice, worked since 1917 as a journalist. He was director and dramaturge in a theatre in Vinohrady, a part of Prague. In the years 1925–1933, he was the first chairman of the Czechoslovakian PEN club. Čapek actively participated in the political and artistic life in Prague and eventually became the most important representative of the cultural life of Czechoslovakia. His works have been translated into several languages. In the thirties, Čapek engaged himself in the battle against the ever strengthening National Socialism. He created theatre plays like *The White Disease* (1937) and *The Mother* (1938) as well as the novel *War with the Newts* (1936). Conspicuous in Čapek's work is his search for a sense of existence and a more profound realisation.

Other important works:
Rossum's Universal Robots (1920)
The Absolute at Large (1922)
Krakatit (1924)

Rainer Maria Rilke (1875–1926) was born in Prague. After finishing from a military school, the lyricist and narrator studied history of art, of literature and legal history in Prague and Berlin, to mention a few. His homeland Bohemia is often the focus of his early poetry and narrations. As opposed to Franz Kafka, Rilke left Prague in his early days. He settled down in Worpswede with the sculptress Clara Westhoff until 1902 and after the marital break-up, he began to lead an unstable life filled with numerous journeys. Among others, his works reflect his stays in Paris where he was Auguste Rodin's secretary in 1905/1906 and in the Mediterranean Duino with Princess Marie of Thurn and Taxis.

Important works:
Larenopfer (1896)
Two Prague Stories (1898)
The Book of Images (1902)
The Notebook of Malte Laurids Brigge (1910)
Duino Elegies (1922)

The Castle District
[Hradčany]

Prague Castle Guards in their becoming uniforms.

A Visit to the Castle District
[Hradčany]

1

The old imperial stronghold (Prague Castle) and the adjoining Castle District [Hradčany] are situated on an elongated rocky hill on the left bank of the River Vltava. The name of the district is derived from the Czech term "hrad" meaning castle. Apart from the extended Castle Courtyards, the Royal Gardens and the Summer Residence "Belvedere", the former suburbs including the impressive Strahov Monastery also belong to this district. The influential gentlemen of the country erected their palaces in this distinguished quarter, in close proximity to the king. The Martinic, Černín, Lobkowicz, Rosenberg, Schwarzenberg and Dietrichstein families lived there at eye-level with his Majesty the Emperor. The building plots in the Castle District became scarce in the 17th century, hence the nobility was forced to move towards the foot of the hill, to the Lesser Town [Malá Strana].

The beginnings of the Prague Castle lead back to the 9th century when the first Christian Přemyslid ruler Bořivoj I moved his capital from Levý Hradec, situated north of Prague, to the banks of the Vltava (875). The establishment, a wooden castle protected by ramparts and a moat, received a stone church consecrated to the Holy Virgin Mary a few years later (890). Bořivoj's son Vratislav I had another church erected in place of the present St George's Basilica. After Prague's establishment as a bishopric (973) the Castle also served as the bishop's seat during the reign of Boleslav II.

Emperor Charles IV of Luxembourg made the Castle that had fallen to ruin during the times of Přemysl Otakar II into the focal point of the Holy Roman Empire. This is where the Gothic St Vitus Cathedral was erected in 1344 when the city was elevated to an archbishopric.

After several years of decline following the Hussite wars, towards the end of the 15th century the Jagiellonian kings moved back to the Castle with their resplendent life and activity since they deemed it necessary to leave the unsafe royal seat in the city after the rebellions in Prague in 1483. The Habsburgs (since 1526) surrounded the structure with gardens, built the splendid Summer Residence "Belvedere" and transformed the dreary stronghold into a comfortable Castle.

The fire in 1541 that devastated the Lesser Town and the Castle District left a breach in the medieval character of the town. But at the same time, the necessary construction and reconstruction that followed helped in the final breakthrough of the already proclaimed Renaissance period.

The stronghold underwent a renewed blossoming under Rudolph II, the legendary Emperor who made Prague into the cultural and political focus of the Holy Roman Empire one last time. The collector, patron of arts and builder had a series of architectural extensions built (for example, the north wing with the Spanish Hall and the Rudolph Gallery) and had a deer enclosure installed in the moat behind the Castle, also the stone Lion Courtyard, a pheasantry, a fishpond as well as a summer riding school.

In 1618 the signal for the estates rebellion and Thirty Years' War is believed to have been given from the Prague Castle, the so-called Second Defenestration of Prague. The imperial governors Jaroslav Martinic and Vilém of Slavata along with their secretary Phillipus Fabricius

were thrown out from a window of the Bohemian Chancellery. In the course of the thus provoked Thirty Years' War the stronghold was occupied by a Saxon and a Swedish Army. Valuable artistic treasures from the Rudolphine Collections were either lost or destroyed.

Had Emperor Rudolph II elevated the complete quarter to royal district thus 150 years later, Maria Theresa declared this "Castle District" as the fourth district of Prague.

In connection with Maria Theresa's wars of succession, the stronghold was damaged several times by besieging armies (a French-Saxon Army in 1741, the Prussians in 1744 and 1757) but also boisterous celebrations in the 18th century: the canonisation of John of Nepomuk (1721), the festivities at the coronation of Charles VI as King of Bohemia (1711) and finally the enthronement of Maria Theresa (1743), the ultimately victorious and

The Castle District seen from Petřín Hill.

Pražský hrad ✈ Prague Castle

A 1188108 12.10.2006 1

okruh | *route*
číslo | *no.*
dne | *date*
plně | *full*
snížené | *reduced*
služby | *services*
cena | *price* 350 KČ

Tisk PEGAS

Platnost dva dny. | *Valid for two days.*

Správa Pražského hradu

Správa Pražského hradu, 11908 Praha1-Hrad, tel.:+420224371111, IČ:49366076, DIC:CZ49366076, www.hrad.cz

❶ Starý královský palác / Old Royal
Palace / Alter Königspalast / Ancien
palais royal / Antico palazzo reale

❷ Příběh Pražského hradu / The Story of
Prague Castle / Die Geschichte der Prager
Burg / l'Histoire du Château de Prague /
La Storia del Castello di Praga

Bazilika sv. Jiří / Basilica of St.
George / St-Georgsbasilika / Basilique
Saint-Georges / Basilica San Giorgio

❸ Národní galerie / National Gallery /
Nationalgalerie / Galerie Nationale /
Galleria Nazionale

❹ Zlatá ulička / Golden Lane /
Goldenes Gässchen / Ruelle d'or / Vicolo d'oro

❹ Obrazárna Pražského hradu / Prague Castle Picture Gallery / Gemäldegalerie
der Prager Burg / Galerie du Château / Pinacoteca del Castello

Strahov Monastery.

acclaimed Empress after bitter battles concerning the succession.

During the reign of her son Joseph II, not only were the remaining treasures from the collections of Rudolph II auctioned but extensive damage was also done through the thoughtless quartering of soldiers, for example in the Royal Summer Residence, the St George's Convent and the Royal Riding School and the large Ball Game Hall.

But an Emperor was to live in this Castle sunk in a fairytale dream yet one last time: the unfortunate Emperor Ferdinand I (known as the kind-hearted one) who since his abdication of the throne in 1848 found, in the seclusion of the Prague Castle, his permanent resting place faraway from the court of Vienna.

After 1918 the president of the young Czechoslovakian Republic, Tomáš Garrigue Masaryk, held office at the Castle, the seat of the country's governing authority. The entire Prague Castle was reconstructed to suit the requirements of the Presidential Chancellery. In 1920 the Slovene architect

Josip Plečnik began remodelling the Castle Gardens and courtyard as well as the president's residence and the representation rooms. The reconstruction and research work carry on even into present times.

Since 1993, the president of the Czech Republic officiates from the Prague Castle.

Strahov Monastery
[Strahovský klášter, Strahovské nádvoří 1, Praha 1]

In 1148, King Vladislav I had a monastery built on the foothills of the Petřín Hill at the gates of the town. The monastery building, originally made of wood, was towed by the Premonstratensian monks from Steinfeld in the Eifel region. In the course of centuries, after numerous alterations and extensions, this Premonstratensian monastery developed into one of the most significant religious centres and the richest abbey in the country, into a place of arts and sciences.

In the 13th century a great fire left the monastery in ash and debris and in the course of the following centuries Strahov was damaged many times as a result of violent events (Hussite wars, the Thirty Years' War, the Prussian siege).

From the Scene of the Fire [Pohořelec] a ramp-like driveway leads unto the portals and into the monastery courtyard. To the right of the archway, the last buttress of a wall erected during the reign of Charles IV are visible, the so-called Hunger Wall owing its name to the circumstances when the destitute people of Prague found work due to it and had bread during the hunger period. The **statue of St Norbert** made by Johann Anton Quittainer in 1755 overlooks the coats of arms adorned portal structure facing the west.

In a courtyard behind the monastery, on an Ionic pillar between the old trees is another statue of the St Norbert who receives special reverence as the founder of the order of this monastery.

Two places of worship in the monastery courtyard merit our attention: to the left of the entrance is the parish church and burial chapel **St Roch** donated by Emperor Rudolph II as a gesture of gratitude for salvation from the plague at the beginning of the 17th century. The shapes are late Gothic but the portal with the winged angel's head signifies the approaching Renaissance. This church is desancitfied and now used as a venue for exhibitions. The second and by far more impressive church is the **Church of the Assumption** with its magnificent features. The originally Romanesque basilica was transferred

Portal of the Strahov Monastery.

Strahov: Statue of St Norbert of Prémontre in the monastery courtyard.

Adjacent to the church is the new **library building** constructed from 1782 to 1784 according to the plans made by Ignaz Palliardi. The interesting classicist façade indicates the spirit imbued with the strivings for enlightenment of the Freemasons Abbot, Wenzel Mayer. The medallion of Ignaz Michael Platzer in the tympanum shows Emperor Joseph II, who sanctioned the construction of this building even though he had ordered the suppression of numerous monasteries in other places.

Due to conservational reasons, tourists are not permitted to enter the Philosophical Hall of the library containing 50,000 books and thus cannot closely view the marvellous ceiling fresco painted in lucid colours depicting the history of the intellect. The then 70 year-old Baroque master Franz Anton Maulbertsch created within a span of just six months in 1794, a truly unique series of paintings. The walnut wood furniture originates from the south Moravian Louka monastery near Znojmo that was suppressed in the course of the Josephine Reform. The white monks were spared the Emperor's reformist zeal. In 1953 the last canons had to eventually leave the monastery to the atheist government for many decades. Since then however, the members of the order have returned to Strahov.

into Baroque by Anselmo Lurago in the mid 18th century; the church towers visible from afar also received their final shape in those days.

In 1744 Johann Anton Quittainer created, for the façade of this monastery church, a young vital Immaculata figure that is described as one of the significant masterpieces of Baroque sculpture in Prague.

During the Thirty Years' War, the mortal remains of the founder of the Premonstatensian order and former Bishop of Magdeburg, Norbert of Prémontre were brought to Prague and buried in this church. In the southern chapel to the right of the main entrance rests the defeated imperial commander-in-chief the Count of Pappenheim, who fell in 1632 near Lützen and who became immortal through the saying "Thus I recognize my Pappenheimers" (from Schiller's *Wallenstein*). Besides many other treasures in the church's interior is the great organ on which Mozart is believed to have played in 1787.

Through a connecting passage in which a copy of the *Strahov Evangel* is preserved, one arrives at the

In the Strahov Monastery courtyard.

Theological Hall of the library, the even older tract of which was built by the master builder Giovanni Domenico Orsi de Orsini.

This hall derives its name from the mainly theological content of the 16,000 books here.

The stucco work on the hall ceiling was painted by a member of the order Frater Siardus Nosecký between 1723 and 1727. Geographical and astronomical globes are placed in the centre of this hall.

The inner monastery area is accessible through a gate decorated with coats of arms situated to the east of the monastery church. In a recess over the gable greets the statue of St Norbert once again. Through the common courtyard, one arrives at the former chapter hall and further on in the **Strahov Picture Gallery** where works of old masters of Baroque (Peter Brandl, Wenzel Lorenz Reiner, Václav Kupetzky and Karel Škréta) are exhibited.

Philosophical Hall of the library.

Pohořelec

[Pohořelec, Praha 1]

The Scene of Fire [Pohořelec] including Strahov and a part of the Petřín Hill were integrated in the Castle District only during the rule of Charles IV. The often contested district due to its strategic importance had been devastated more than once in conflagrations, in the battles between the Hussites and King Sigismund's Imperial Army in 1420, during the great fire in the Castle suburb in 1541 and in the battles between Austrians and French troops in 1742. This somewhat sleepy suburban quarter is a picturesque city square surrounded by beautiful buildings from the later Renaissance period with several interesting Baroque and rococo façades.

The **Nepomuk statue** at the square was created in 1752 by Johann Anton Quittainer. It stood at the Castle Square until 1846.

The **Kutschera Palace** [Pohořelec 22] is a rococo building from the second half of the 18th century. The former owner Field Marshall Lt Baron of Kutschera was, amongst others, acquainted with Ludwig van Beethoven and even occasionally accompanied the violin-playing Emperor Francis I on the flute.

In "**The Broad Courtyard**" [Pohořelec 26] lived the Czech painter Mikoláš Aleš.

The Renaissance building "**At the Golden Tree**" [Pohořelec 8] is conspicuous due to the double gabled roof. A staired passageway leads into the courtyard of the Strahov Monastery.

A look at the Scene of Fire from the Strahov ramp.

Černín Palace

3

[Černínský palác,
Loretánské náměstí 5, Praha 1]

Count Humprecht Johann of Černín obtained an ideal plot for a representational family palace in 1666. Three and a half storeys were planned spread over a breadth of thirty columns. Three entrance-ways emphasise the symmetry of this imposing palace that dominates the dainty Loretto Square like a potentate's fortress. The architect Francesco Caratti was in charge of construction until his death in 1677 and the master builder Giovanni de Capauli often employed more than a hundred masons and craftsmen simultaneously at this large construction site.

Although the successors carried on with the construction after the demise of Humprecht Johann of Černín in 1697, the palace remained unfinished and could never be used as the family seat of the Černíns.

After severe damages during the Bavarian-French occupation (1742) and also the Prussian siege (1744, 1757), the owners tried to sell the colossus to Emperor Joseph II – but without success.

In 1851, the military acquired the palace that had already served as a military hospital during the Napoleonic wars and converted it into barracks. The palace was extravagantly restored after 1918 and finally devoted anew to representational purposes: the Ministry of Foreign Affairs of the young republic pitched its tents in Černín Palace. It happened to be the seat of

Ministry of Foreign Affairs: Černín Palace.

the Reich Protector from 1939 to 1944.

In March 1948, the year of the coup, the then Minister of Foreign Affairs, Jan Masaryk, was found dead beneath one of the windows of the palace. The circumstances of his death have not been clarified to date; people even speak when referring to it as the Third Defenestration of Prague.

The Ministry of Foreign Affairs is based in the Černín Palace again. The Palace Garden adorned with statues of Giovanni Santini-Aichel is only open to the public for concerts and theatre performances in summer.

Loretto Shrine

[Loreta,
Loretánské náměstí 7, Praha 1]

According to a legend, the house where the Virgin Mary was heralded the approaching birth of the saviour was threatened by heathens, so it was carried by angels from Nazareth to the small town of Loretto near Ancona. This pious motive was adopted on several occasions, especially in the Baroque period, and gave cause to the founding of places of pilgrimage all over Europe. Fifty such shrines were erected in Bohemia alone.

The best known of such Loretto Shrines, the Loretto Shrine in Prague, was founded by the Countess Benigna Katherina of Lobkowicz who came from a well-to-do Bohemian family. The attractive west façade adorned with elaborate relief ornaments by Kilian Ignaz Dientzenhofer with the (ancient) octagonal belfry originates from the years 1721/22.

Eberhard of Glachau, a Prague trader had the **chime** with 27 bells cast in Amsterdam for 15,000 Guilders in 1694. The Prague clockmaker Peter Naumann set it in motion in the presence of noted clergy and nobility. It rings out the hymn *We Greet Thee a Thousand Times* on the hour.

Casa Santa, the Lorettan House in the courtyard of the complex is the centre of the shrine. Cloisters were built around Casa Santa after 1661 and the pilgrims singing the Lorettan litany moved from altar to altar through them.

Loretto Shrine in wintertime.

The Bearded Virgin.

In the **Chapel of the Grievous Virgin Mary** is a peculiar cult image: a bearded woman nailed to the cross. St Wilgefortis had refused to marry the chosen heathen and prayed for visible signs of masculinity to rescue her virginity, is portrayed here. The enraged father had his recalcitrant daughter nailed to the cross.

The **Church of the Nativity** built by father and son Dientzenhofer, a precious jewel of Prague Baroque, received its present appearance in about 1735. The ceiling is painted with frescoes by Wenzel Lorenz Reiner (*Offering Jesus in the Temple* and *Worship by the Three Holy Kings; Worship by the Shepherds*).

The valuable Loretto Treasure in the **Treasure Room** can be traced back to largely gifts from wealthy noble families. Though the treasure is decimated by losses due to the wars, the circa 300 jewels, trinkets, gems, liturgical utensils and elaborate monstrance delight even fastidious art lovers.

The oldest object on display is a late Gothic chalice from 1510, the most valuable object in the collection is the so-called **Diamond Monstrance** ("Prague Sun"). The latter was made by royal Viennese jewellers in 1699 based on the design of Johann Bernhard Fischer von Erlach. The gilded silver monstrance weighing 12 kg is set with 6,222 diamonds. A dragon is depicted at the foot of the monstrance symbolising the powers of darkness and evil. On a half-moon stands the Queen of Heaven Maria Immaculata crowned by 12 stars. She looks at the radiant sun that symbolises God as the light of the world.

Façade detail of Loretto Church.

Capuchin monastery in Prague.

Capuchin Monastery with the Church of St Mary
[Klášter kapucínů s kostelem Panny Marie, Loretánské náměstí 6, Praha 1]

This monastery founded in 1601 was the first Capuchin monastery in Bohemia. In the connected **Church of Our Dear Lady to the Angels** that conforms in its plainness to the order's indigence ideal, is a beautiful statue of St Mary. A Baroque nativity

scene with almost life-size figures is set up in an adjacent room at Christmastime.

New World
[Nový Svět, Praha 1]

In the 16th century, on the northern outskirts of the Castle District, over the trench of the Brusnice stream, emerged a frugal settlement: the New World. Although the small houses in the little lane were burned down many times in the course of centuries, the district has nevertheless retained its romantic charm. The people living here were certainly not wealthy but they were fortunate to have a roof over their heads. What a wonder that they endorsed their dwellings with the proud attribute "golden"! The picturesque New World has, in the meantime,

Then and now in the New World.

House "At the Golden Grape".

become a distinguished artist's quarter and its tranquillity is a pleasant contrast to the lively bustle of the Golden Lane.

> The Baroque house "**At the Golden Plough**" [Nový Svět 25] originates from the 17th century. The Czech violin virtuoso František Ondříček was born here in 1857.
>
> The house "**At the White Lion**" [Nový Svět 21] has a very beautiful ivy covered inner courtyard.
>
> The house "**At the Golden Grape**" [Nový Svět 5] originates from the 17th century and is guarded by a fierce looking predatory fish on the bay.
>
> The house "**At the Golden Pear**" [Nový Svět 3], is a Baroque structure from the 18th century and houses a traditional tavern to which the façade adornment relates: ears of corn and grapevines stand for food and drink.
>
> The imperial astronomer Tycho de Brahe is supposed to have lived in "**At the Golden Griffin**" [Nový Svět 1].

Church of St John of Nepomuk at the Prague Castle

7

[Kostel sv. Jana z Nepomuku, Kanovnická, Praha 1]

This is the first church to be erected on a cruciform plan by the Baroque architect Kilian Ignaz Dientzenhofer in Prague between 1720 and 1728. The ceiling frescoes by Wenzel Lorenz Reiner demonstrate scenes from the life of St Nepomuk.

This place of worship with its appertaining Ursuline convent was closed down in the course of the Josephine Reform and was later used as a garrison church (since 1902) and even barracks. A prominent officer in the barracks was the Imperial and Royal Colonel Crown Prince Rudolph of Habsburg who served as Commandant of the Infantry Regiment n° 36 since 1879.

Kanovnická Lane

8

[Kanovnická, Praha 1]

The **Austrian residence** [Kanovnická 4] is in a medieval building built in the Renaissance style around

Austrian ambassador's official residence.

1600 and remodelled to Baroque around 1690 by the Captain of the Castle, Albrecht Hložek of Žampach. The palace with its beautiful gardens accommodates the official residence of the ambassador of the Austrian Republic. In the magnificent reception rooms, the brilliance of old Austria can be felt on special occasions even today.

The sgraffitoed **House of Pages** [Kanovnická 3] was used as accommodation for the Imperial Pages.

Castle Square
[Hradčanské náměstí, Praha 1]

The **Marian column** at the centre of the Castle Square was made in 1726 and placed there as a plague column in 1736. The holy figures overlooking the Immaculata – John of Nepomuk, Elizabeth, Peter, Norbert, Florian, Charles

Borromeus, Wenceslas, Vitus and Adalbert – originate from Ferdinand Maximilian Brokoff's workshop.

The **Tuscany Palace** [Hradčanské náměstí 5] was owned by the Dukes of Tuscany since 1718. At the corner to the Loretto Lane is a Baroque group of sculptures that depicts Archangel Michael with the flaming sword. Above each of the two portals of this two axled building are prominently displayed ducal coat of arms crowned with a cornucopia.

The **Martinic Palace** [Hradčanské náměstí 8] was built by Jaroslav Bořita of Martinic who was one of the victims of the defenestration from the Bohemian Chancellery. Renaissance-sgraffitos show scenes from the Bible and classical mythology.

In the **Canon's Residence** [Hradčanské náměstí 10] lived the Swabian cathedral master builder Peter Parler who was entrusted with the construction of St Vitus Cathedral by Emperor

View of the Castle Square from St Vitus Cathedral.

Archbishop's Palace.

ted to the neighbouring Schwarzenberg Palace.

The **Schwarzenberg Palace** [Hradčanské náměstí 2] was built by Johann Count Lobkowicz in the Florentine style between 1545 and 1563. An Army Museum was accommodated in this sgraffitoed palace for several years, now the National Gallery has found a home here.

The **Carmelite Convent** [Hradčanské náměstí 3] belongs to the barefooted Carmelites since 1792.

Charles IV after the death of the first builder Matthew of Arras.

The **Sternberg Palace** [Hradčanské náměstí 15] can be reached through an entrance adjacent to the Archbishop's Palace. Wenzel Adalbert Count Sternberg had this simple four-winged complex built in the years 1695–1720.

The **Archbishop's Palace** [Hradčanské náměstí 16] is a late Baroque palace based on a Renaissance structure. Sculptures by Ignaz Franz Platzer, five balconies and a coat of arms adorn the impressive front façade. The Archbishops of Prague reside here since 1562.

The **Salm Palace** [Hradčanské náměstí 1] is the empire palace connec-

Royal Gardens 10
[Královské zahrady, Pražský hrad, Praha 1]

Through a wrought-iron gate opposite the Riding School (adjacent to the Lion Courtyard, formerly a cage for predatory animals), one arrives in the Royal Gardens. Old vineyards were replaced by greenery by the Emperor Ferdinand I and his successors in the 16th century and now exude the charm of an English Park. In the beginning, when the first tulips in Central Europe blossomed here, the Royal Gardens were a Renaissance paradise and even in the Baroque 18th century the gardens blossomed until the idyll was destroyed in the times of war.

The first building to the right, surrounded by chestnut trees, is the **Presidential Residence**. A greenhouse built by Kilian Ignaz Dientzenhofer was extended through side-aisles towards the end of the 1940s. A short distance ahead is the sgraffitoed Royal **Ball Game Hall** [Míčovna] built between 1567 and 1569, formerly an open loggia structure by Bonifaz Wol-

Schwarzenberg Palace.

Royal Ball Game Hall.

mut. In the intermediate neighbourhood is the **Orangery** vaulted by a plain glass and steel construction.

Royal Summer Residence "Belvedere" 11
[Letohrádek královny Anny, Pražský hrad, Praha 1]

This marvellous summer palace was a gift from Emperor Ferdinand I to his wife Anna Jagiello.

It was begun in 1534 and completed in a construction period of more than two decades in the Lombardic Renaissance style.

The passage arcades are decorated with numerous ornate reliefs and coats of arms depicting scenes from classical mythology and national history. The interior of this summer palace conceals two domed Renaissance halls on the ground floor and a dance hall with a wooden coffered ceiling upstairs. This room has wall panels with themes from the Bohemian national history.

In front of the Palace "Belvedere" used as exhibition rooms nowadays, the **Singing Fountain** cast in 1568 attracts the attention of strollers. Its name is derived not from the bagpiper throned on the fountain's centre but the sound the falling water drops produce on impact with the bronze fountain bowls. Scenes from antique mythology are depicted at the foot of the fountain.

Summer Residence „Belvedere" in the Royal Gardens.

Prague Castle

[Pražský hrad]

Prague Castle
[Pražský hrad, Praha 1]

In the First Castle Courtyard `12`

Matthew Gate at the entrance to the Second Castle Courtyard.

The so-called **Courtyard of Honour** can be entered through a wrought-iron gate with the monograms of the Empress Maria Theresa and her son Joseph II, guarded by two regiment guards. The two battling Titans flanking the gate were carved by the rococo sculptor Ignaz Franz Platzer in 1770; the original sculptures were replaced by copies in 1921. The building wings originate from the second half of the 18th century and mark in their austerity the end of Prague Baroque. At that time, after the Seven Years' War against the Prussians, Empress Maria Theresa entrusted the Viennese architect Nicolo Pacassi with the reconstruction of the Imperial Palace.

The **Matthew Gate** (1614) is considered the earliest example of Prague Baroque. Emperor Matthew I entrusted the famous Italian master builder Vincenzo Scamozzi with its construction. The Theresian architect had the gate previously belonging to the stronghold complex integrated in the entrance tract. The slim flagpoles flanking the portals make us aware for the first time of the world of shapes of the Slovene architect Josip Plečnik.

From the passage to the Second Castle Courtyard, a stately staircase on the right leads to the **representation rooms**, the erstwhile Imperial Chambers. To the left, a newer staircase leads to one of the porticos designed by Josip Plečnik. From here one can access other stately rooms, for example, the Rothmayer Hall, the Spanish Hall and the Rudolph

Giant at the Castle Portal.

Gallery. Most of the representation rooms however are not accessible to the public. Only a select few are permitted the viewing of the Throne Hall, the Habsburg-, Brožík-, Mirror-, Music-, Social- or Čermák Salons.

In the Second Castle Courtyard 13

The early Baroque **sandstone fountain** in the Second Courtyard stems from the Prague stonemasons Hieronymus Kohl and the Italian Francesco della Torre. Until 1918, this fountain at the feet of the four Roman gods (Vulcanus, Hercules, Neptune, and Mercury) was crowned by an imperial eagle.

Fountain in the Castle Courtyard.

> In later years (1961–1990), the treasure of St Vitus Cathedral was stored in the Chapel of the Holy Cross. This late Baroque place of worship was built by Anselmo Lurago who based it on the plans of the court architect Pacassi.
> In the 19th century the chapel was reconstructed in a classicist manner. The chapel's interior, painted and adorned with biblical motives, and especially the crucifixion painting at the altar is worth mentioning.

The Chapel of the Holy Cross was the family chapel of the unfortunate monarch Ferdinand I who, since his abdication in 1848 lived at the Prague Castle in quiet seclusion.

On the opposite side is the entrance to the Castle Gallery where significant works from the imperial collections are exhibited (Rubens, Tintoretto, Titian and Veronese, to name a few). The Rudolphine Stables to the north are also utilised for exhibition purposes.

In the Third Castle Courtyard St Vitus Cathedral 14
[Chrám sv. Víta, Pražský hrad, Praha 1]

In the 11th century, in place of the Romanesque rotunda, a three nave basilica that would serve the Přemyslid dynasty as the coronation and burial church was constructed. In 1344 Emperor Charles IV entrusted the French architect Matthew of Arras with the construction of the Gothic cathedral. After his death in 1352, the building work was set forth by the Swabian Peter Parler with a substantially altered fundamental conception. The Hussite wars brought the construction to a standstill in 1419. Its completion was to follow only in the 20th century by the cathedral master builders Kamil Hilbert and Josef Mocker in neo-Gothic style. The official opening ceremony of the 124 m long cathedral took place in 1929.

The west front of the cathedral is adorned with statues and is overlooked by two 82 m high neo-Gothic spires. The bishop's church can be entered through three exquisitely detailed portals with relief decorated bronze doors.

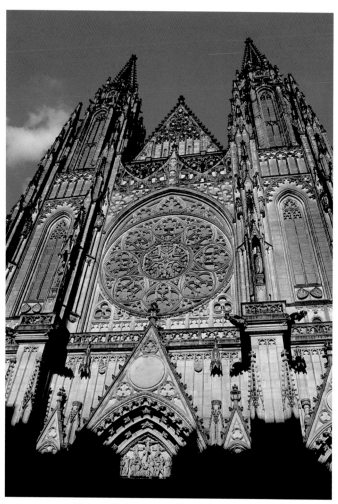

The neo-Gothic towers of the St Vitus Cathedral.

Bust of Charles IV at the triforium.

The interior offers the visitor an impressive panorama of the Gothic cathedral; the neo-Gothic construction in the area of the nave passes over almost seamlessly into the medieval section of the choir bathed in warm light.

In front of the neo-Gothic high altar in the choir loft of the St Vitus Cathedral and the ornamental Baroque choir stalls is the **Royal Mausoleum** made of white marble in 1589. It is surrounded by a particularly artistically forged Renaissance lattice. The individual parts of the mausoleum were produced in Innsbruck and were transported to Prague by sledge and over waterways. The royal majesties resting on the tomb are presented in rich detail: the Habsburg Ferdinand I flanked by his wife Anna Jagiello and his son Maximilian II. The relief medallions on the side walls show the rulers who were formerly buried under the mausoleum: Charles IV (with wives), Wenceslas IV, Ladislav Postumus and George of Poděbrady.

The national coat of arms painted on the arcade walls conveys an impression of the expansion of the Habsburg hereditary land in the 17th century.

From the inner and outer **triforium** of the nave and the choral loft, several dozens of animal heads, mascarones and extraordinary portraits of important personalities looked down at the beholder, among them the famous portraits of Emperor Charles IV and his wives as well as a bust of the cathedral's master builders Peter Parler and Matthew of Arras. It would fill a far more extensive publication if one wanted to describe in detail the art treasures and peculiarities of the various chapels of the St Vitus Cathedral (the **St Sigismund Chapel** with the relics of the holy Sigismund, the **St Nepomuk Chapel** opposite the silver monument of the holy Nepomuk designed by Fischer von Erlach, the **Pernstein Chapel** which is the burial chapel of the Archbishops of Prague, the Chapel of the Holy Cross with access to the royal crypt, the **St Anna Chapel** opposite the relief carving by Georg Bendl with the portrayal of the flight of the winter king Frederick of the Palatinate after the Battle of the White Mountain, the **Saxon Chapel** with the tombs of the Kings Přemysl Otakar I and II, the **Waldstein Chapel** with the crypt of the famous Bohemian noble family Waldstein etc. The most important chapel certainly is the high Gothic **St Wenceslas Chapel**.)

Statue of St Wenceslas at
the St Wenceslas Chapel.

The burial chapel of St Wenceslas is splendidly decorated and contains several extremely valuable works of art.

Wenceslas I, whose dead body was brought to the St Vitus Rotunda at the orders of his brother (and murderer) Boleslav I, had while he was still alive, expressed the wish to be buried in this church after his death. Peter Parler erected the luxurious chapel on the grave of the holy one at the orders of Emperor Charles IV. The chapel walls between the cornice and the base are adorned with the valuable murals and gilded stucco decorations as well as more than 1,300 emeralds and semi precious stones in all colours.

Two portals lead into the chapel. The wrought-iron portal to the west made in the 20th century contrasts with the Gothic portal on the north with the sculptural adornments made by Peter Parler. Another noteworthy door is in the chapel's interior: the entrance to the **Crown Chamber** equipped with seven locks where the

coronation insignia of the Bohemian kings (crown, imperial orb and sceptre) are stored. The coronation insignia are exhibited and viewable for the public only on rare occasions. This has taken place merely eight times in the 20th century.

Through the **Hasenburg Chapel** situated to the south, one arrives at the spiral staircase that leads to the upper tower level and to the bells. The panorama from the top is unique! It pays not to shy away from a narrow stairwell with 285 stairs solely for this incredible view. On the southern exterior of the cathedral is the impressive large copper topped St Vitus belfry. The Renaissance master builder Bonifaz Wolmut lent it the characteristic roof shape. Behind a lancet window with a gilded ornamental grille hangs, since 1549, the heaviest bell in the country with its

St Vitus Cathedral belfry.

St Vitus Cathedral at night
(choir with chapels).

18 tons in weight – the name "Sigismund" was chosen for it.

The crowned "R" above the window reminds one of the Habsburg Emperor Rudolph II who was surrounded by legends and whose fate is so closely connected to that of the Prague Castle. Three stone coats of arms are fixed beneath the window: to the left, the two tailed Bohemian lion, in the centre the flame eagle of St Wenceslas (the Bohemian heraldic beast of older times) and to the right the archbishop's coat of arms. From the two dials, with just one hand each, one can read the time: the topmost dial shows the hours and the lower dial the minutes and quarters of an hour.

Adjacent to the belfry is the world famous Golden Gate (Porta aurea) leading to the Cathedral's interior. A glass mosaic created by the Venetian craftsmen at the instruction of Emperor Charles IV sparkles in 30 different colours over three pointed arches. The mosaic reminds the beholder of the Last Judgement and the blazing flames of purgatory. A delegation of Bohemian patron saints looks up at the saviour. Emperor Charles IV and his wife Elizabeth of Pomerania – in the spandrel beneath – also attend court. From the Cathedral Square, the bull stairs of Josip Plečnik grant entry to the **South Gardens** (Rampart and Paradise Gardens). The garden complexes offer an abundance of sightseeing details and great views of the historical city centre. Plečnik conjured up a unique garden world with fountains, pavilions, steps, lawns, pyramids, obelisks – one can spend hours studying the characteristic shapes of the Slovene castle architect and enjoying the interplay of art and nature.

Old Provosty

15

[Staré proboštství,
Pražský hrad, Praha 1]

On the southwest corner of the St Vitus Cathedral is the Old Provosty of the cathedral chapter, the former seat of the bishops in Prague. The building originates from the 18th century, though the

The Old Provosty.

statue of St Wenceslas at the corner of the building is older (1662); it is the work of the leading Prague Baroque sculptor and carver of those times, Johann Georg Bendl.

Plečnik's Obelisk 16
[Plečnikův obelisk,
Pražský hrad, Praha 1]

In 1928, on the tenth anniversary of the foundation of the republic, an almost 17 m high obelisk was erected opposite the Old Provosty in memory of the victims of the World War. The architect Josip Plečnik chose an enormous block of Mrákotín granite for the obelisk. His original plan, to set up an allegorical sculpture and to lay a Grave for the Unknown Soldier at the foot of the column could not be implemented. The monument has till today remained only a torso.

St George's Statue 17
[Socha sv. Jiří,
Pražský hrad, Praha 1]

The statue of St George on horseback created by the brothers Martin and Georg of Klausenburg in 1373 is the most important sculpture in the Third Castle Courtyard. The statue is however only a copy. It stands on a diorite plinth by Josip Plečnik. The original statue is in the nearby St George's Convent. The saint's horse that looks as if it is about to slay a dragon with its lance was destroyed in a tournament in 1562 and so we cannot be certain if the replica corresponds exactly to the original.

A sheltered archaeological site is visible opposite the statue of St George. In the course of extensive earthmoving, valuable old stonework that is not allowed to be covered up again was discovered in the 1920s. This concerned the foundation walls of the former Bishop's Chapel St Mauritius and the St Vitus Basilica from the 11th century. Josip Plečnik created an iron concrete construction that safeguards the area.

Old Royal Palace 18
[Starý královský palác,
Jiřské náměstí 33, Praha 1]

The origins of this palace go back to the 1st century AD. The complicated architectonic construction

Statue of St George.

of the building impressively mirrors the style epochs of past centuries.

Through the entrance hall one arrives at the representation floor on the same ground level. After a glance in the **"Green Chamber"** on the left, where the royal court was held and in the small audience hall (the so-called "King's Bedchamber") awaits a special sight; the **Vladislav Hall** created by the Austrian Benedikt von Ried around 1500 on the threshold to Renaissance. The Throne Hall has been the scene of many a ceremonial meeting and this is the palace where many a great one of the nation mounted his steed at a jousting tournament. Even today, the splendid vaulted hall serves as a representative scene for ceremonial occasions, be it the elections for the President of the

The so-called Bohemian Chancellery.

republic or noble receptions for important state guests.

From the southwest corner of the Vladislav Hall, one arrives in the so-called Louis Tract with the two **Bohemian Chancellery** rooms. Through a crowned portal bearing the initial L for Louis Jagiello, one steps into a historical room: on 23rd May 1618, two

Vladislav Hall in the Old Royal Palace.

imperial governors were plunged into the depths from a window in the east wall of the former Chancellery (Second Defenestration of Prague).

Since about 1600, the Vladislav Hall has been connected to the **All Saints Chapel** by a portal adorned with the coat of arms, the preceding structure of which goes back to the 12th century. After the great fire in 1541 the chapel was rebuilt in its present form and in succession (in 1755) intended as a collegiate church for the noble ladies of the neighbourhood. The Baroque high altar is provided with an altarpiece by Wenzel Lorenz Reiner. The legend of St Procopius is narrated in a pictorial series by Christian Dittmann whose relics were transferred to the Prague Castle in 1588 from the Benedictine monastery Sázava where he was an abbot. The Baroque monument for the saint surrounded by allegories of virtue stands in a recess in the north wall of the chapel. The painting *Deposition from the Cross* on the side-altar to the right is attributed it to the Rudolphine court artist Hans von Aachen.

From the portals on the north of the Vladislav Hall, through a spiral staircase one comes to the coat of arms adorned rooms of the **"New National Plaques"** and in the **Old Common Law Chamber**. After the fire of 1541, Bonifaz Wolmut rebuilt it with very decorative Gothic tracery. During state parliament meetings, the representatives of the estates sat

View of Prague Castle, in the foreground (left of the centre) the Old Royal Palace.

on the upholstered benches, the throne with the Bohemian lions was reserved for the king.

Through the Rider's Staircase with an arched rib-vaulting by Benedikt von Ried which even mounted tournament participants could ride through in the olden days, we leave the Vladislav Hall and the Royal Palace.

St George's Basilica 19
[Kostel sv. Jiří,
Pražský hrad, Praha 1]

The foundation walls of the basilica originate from the 12th century, the brick-red façade from behind which the Romanesque choir towers rise up is however early Baroque. St George the dragon slayer stands guard in the tympanum at the front while on the portal ledge of the chapel built at the beginning of the 18th century, a statue of St Nepomuk looks down at the visitors.

The basilica opens into the Jiřská Lane through an early Renaissance portal from the beginning of the 16th century, once again there is a depiction of St George battling the dragon in the portal's tympanum.

The Přemyslid tombs are to be found in the nave of this Romanesque church interior with the wooden beam ceiling. The founder of this church Vratislav I, deceased in 921 is buried here in a striking tomb.

The painted **Choir Chapel of St Ludmila** is very important because of the grave of St Wenceslas' grandmother. The stone figure on the tomb reminds one of St Ludmila's martyrdom; she was attacked in her widow's home Tetín not far from Prague and was strangled with her veil 925 AD. A cross-vaulted Romanesque **crypt** awaits us beneath the choir loft. An allegory to vanity originating from the 16th century is preserved there: in the decomposing entrails of a human body crawl snakes and revolting swarms of diminutive creatures.

The dome of the **Nepomuk Chapel** towards the exit is painted too: Wenzel Lorenz Reiner portrayed the apotheosis of the saints in 1722. He painted the altar panels for both the altars too. Scenes from the lives of the saints can be viewed on the walls.

St George's Basilica from the tower of St Vitus Cathedral.

Towers of the stronghold fortification: Daliborka (round tower) and Black Tower.

The National Gallery displays a collection of Bohemian Mannerist and Baroque art in the basilica's neighbouring early Baroque convent.

Golden Lane  20
[Zlatá ulička,
Pražský hrad, Praha 1]

The medieval fortified wall of the ditch of the Brusnice stream behind the Castle created the architectonic basis for a small picturesque street, the Goldmakers Lane. Goldsmiths probably lived in the dwellings built beneath the fortified wall in the 15th century hence the name "Goldsmith Lane". The wretched huts and houses were demolished under Rudolph II; as a result the Emperor permitted 24 members of the castle guard to use the blind arcades beneath the battlemented parapet as storerooms.

Over the battlemented parapet whose crenelles enabled defending the Castle from the north in the 15th century, one reaches the so-called **"White Tower"**, an artillery tower at the west end of the Goldmakers Lane. During the rule of Emperor Rudolph II this tower was a dark dungeon; on the ground floor above the dungeons was a torture chamber. The English alchemist and charlatan Edward Kelley belonged to the legendary inmates. Probably the best known resident of the Golden Lane was Franz Kafka who quartered himself in house n° 22 for several months in 1916/17, and amongst others, wrote the narrations of the book *A Country*

The Golden Lane at Prague Castle.

Kafka's little house in Golden Lane (n° 22).

Doctor. A small bookshop has been set up here in his honour. Another artillery tower of the northerly defence complex is the **Dalibor Tower** [Daliborka]. Prisons and deep dark dungeons were made even in this tower rising high above the deer enclosure. The Knight Dalibor of Kozojedy was among those imprisoned here. The unfortunate knight attained fame beyond the country's borders with the romantic opera *Dalibor* by Bedřich Smetana.

Burgrave's Palace **21**
[Purkrabství, Jiřská 4, Praha 1]

The former Burgrave's Palace is situated in the Jiřská Lane. A coat of arms carved in stone over the entrance portal remind one of the families that once occupied this honourable office.

On the extended grounds, close to newer buildings are the main building of the Burgrave County and the **"Black Tower"** that was known as the "Golden Tower" in the Middle Ages due to its gilded lead roof.

Opposite the Supreme Burgrave's Palace one sees the **palace of the Lobkowicz family**, an early Baroque palace in whose magnificent halls concerts and exhibitions are held.

Zde žil Franz Kafka

Façade detail on house n° 22: *Franz Kafka lived here.*

The Old Castle stairway connects the eastern part of the Castle to the Lesser Town.

The Lesser Town
[Malá Strana]

A Walk through the Lesser Town
[Malá Strana]

The narrow lanes, squares and gardens of this picturesque part of the city lie at the foot of two dominant hills: the Castle Hill with the Prague Castle borders the Lesser Town on the north, the wooded Petřín Hill forms the boundary on the south end.

The first signs of settlement in the Lesser Town in the area of the Bridge Lane [Mostecká] and Lesser Town Square [Malostranské náměstí] go back to the first century. Přemysl Otakar II finally established the Lesser Town in 1257, had it fortified and the wall built around it. Under the rule of Charles IV, this part of the city was extended considerably on the south end to Petřín Hill and enclosed by the Hunger Wall built about 1360.

The Lesser Town was devastated during the Hussite wars because it posed as a strategic perimeter for the defence of the castle. The contending sides purposefully destroyed the buildings so that the enemy could not find cover. After the Hussites took over the Prague Castle on 7th July 1421, this part of the city was nothing but an expanse of rubble. The ruins of the Lesser Town of Prague could only be rebuilt and repaired by the extremely decimated citizenry many years later.

When King Vladislav Jagiello moved the royal seat from the Old Town to the Castle again in 1484, the Lesser Town was once again threatened due to its function as a strategic perimeter. But not only were armed conflicts to be feared;

on the afternoon of 2nd June 1541 a fire broke out at the Lesser Town Square rapidly engulfing areas around it and soon developed into the most devastating conflagration in the history of Prague. This fire disaster of 1541 that turned two thirds of the Lesser Town buildings and also large parts of the Prague Castle into debris and ashes entirely changed the appearance of the Lesser Town. The fire ruins were rebuilt in the then reigning Renaissance styles and even the buildings spared by the fire were remodelled according to contemporary taste.

Under the Habsburg crown and especially after the Battle of the White Mountain, the Lesser Town took on an increasingly feudal character. Many unfortunate Protestant noble families had to leave the town but Catholic aristocrats replaced them and settled down primarily in the immediate vicinity of the Imperial Castle. They built mansions and palaces in the Lesser Town and fulfilled their expectations of a representative lifestyle in the quiet lanes. After the misery of the Thirty Years' War, new times had dawned when awareness of life is reflected in the opulent Baroque shapes too. Within one single generation emerged dozens of buildings and art monuments and this period moulded the appearance of the Lesser Town like no other to this day.

2

A look at the wintry Lesser Town (to the right,
the towers of St Nicholas, left St Thomas).

With the approaching end of the 18th century the days of the Baroque period were numbered, the Catholic dominance began to crumble; the nobility lost its supremacy to the strengthened citizens who attained influence and affluence in the course of industrialisation of the 19th century. But the Lesser Town, having integrated to form the union of the four cities of Prague in 1784, transformed itself into a sleepy area of town spared the hustle and bustle of the 19th century and the quiet spell prevails here even today.

Lesser Town Square   22
[Malostranské náměstí, Praha 1]

The Lesser Town Square was known as "Italian Square" in the days of Emperor Rudolph II

Lesser Town Square from
St Nicholas Church belfry.

A look from the Castle
forecourt at the Lesser Town.

View of the Lesser Town, in the background (centre) Strahov Monastery.

and between 1859 and 1918 "Radetzky Square" named after the famous Field Marshall. The square is divided into two halves by the Baroque **St Nicholas Church**.

The **Trinity column** that commemorates the dangers survived during the plague was erected at the upper part of the square in 1715.

The lower part of the square is dominated by the **"Grömling" Palace**

with its magnificent Baroque façade. Since the 19th century the traditional "Café Radetzky" later known as "Malostranská kavárna" was situated here.

The **Kaiserstein Palace** [Malostranské náměstí 23] is decorated with statues of the seasons. A bust commemorates Emma Destinnová, one of Enrico Caruso's partners.

The **Lesser Town City Hall** [Malostranské náměstí 21] was the seat of the Lesser Town self-government until the amalgamation of the four Prague cities.

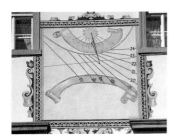

Lesser Town façade details:
A sundial shows the time of day.

Roof and chimney
confusion in the Lesser Town.

St Nicholas Church in the Lesser Town.

The (former) Lesser Town City Hall.

The lively Nerudova Street.

Lichtenstein Palace [Malostranské náměstí 13] a Renaissance building with its classicist façade was the Imperial Governor's seat until 1918.

St Nicholas Church
[Kostel sv. Mikuláše, Malostranské náměstí, Praha 1]

With its impressive dome and the 79 m high belfry, the St Nicholas Church rises in the centre of the Lesser Town Square. This church is the most significant creation of high Baroque in Prague and was built between 1673 and 1755 on behalf of the Jesuits. It is a magnificent masterpiece of the master builders Christoph and Kilian Ignaz Dientzenhofer from Bavaria.

The church interior is decorated with an almost too extravagant splendour. A gilded statue of St Nicholas made by Ignaz Franz Platzer is placed on the high altar, the side altars are fitted with panels of the most important Baroque artists, the nave is painted with arresting frescoes. The ceiling panel in the nave painted on an area of 1,500 m² is one of the largest frescoes in Europe.

Nerudova Street
[Nerudova, Praha 1]

The Nerudova is a driveway from Lesser Town Square up towards the Castle. The steep street bears the name of the important Prague writer Jan Neruda who lived here and found the models for his famous *Prague Tales from the Little Quarter*. Before that the street was known as "Spurs Makers Lane" because of the resident craftsmen. There are still a particularly large number of original Prague house symbols that were commonly used as the address before the present house numbers were introduced.

Well known house symbol in the Nerudova: "At the Three Violins".

The Czech author Jan Neruda.

The **Černín-Morzin Palace** originates from 1670. Both the moor figures (after the family name Morzin) on the portal are from Ferdinand Maximilian Brokoff. This city palace is at present occupied by the Romanian embassy.

The **Thun-Hohenstein Palace** [Nerudova 20] a building made by Giovanni Santini-Aichel (1677 to 1723) impresses with a magnificent Baroque portal with two enormous eagles spreading their wings. The Italian Embassy has been based here since 1921. Adjacent to the palace is the Marian Church of the Theatine order built in 1672. This order was also repealed by Emperor Joseph II. In the house **"At the Golden Lion"** [Nerudova 32] is an apothecary museum.

The legendary advocate Franz Josef of Bretfeld organised glittering balls in the Palace **"At Summer and Winter"** [Nerudova 33]. Mozart and his wife

Konstanze were also the guests here in 1787.

The house **"At the Red Lion"** [Nerudova 45] does not have its own entranceway. To reach inside the building it is necessary to go through the adjacent house.

In the house **"At the Two Suns"** [Nerudova 47] lived the Czech poet Jan Neruda.

Waldstein Palace and Garden
[Valdštejnský palác a zahrada, Valdštejnské náměstí, Praha 1]

One of the largest building projects in the Lesser Town was the palace of the Imperial Generalissimo Albrecht of Waldstein. He obtained a wide expanse of land in the neighbourhood of the Augustine monastery in the 1620s

Front view of the Waldstein Palace.

The Sala terrena of the Waldstein Palace.

Bronze horse in the Waldstein Garden.

have found an almost ideal installation spot to replace the originals that were transported by the Swedish troops to their homeland during the Thirty Years' War. The Senate of the Czech Republic occupies the Waldstein Palace that has been adapted for this purpose.

Church and Monastery 26 St Thomas

[Kostel a klášter sv. Tomáše, Letenská, Praha 1]

and had a many-winged palace in late Renaissance style built at the site. 23 buildings, a brickyard and several gardens had to go to make way for the complex. The complex consists of three courtyards and an elongated garden. The **Waldstein Stables** constantly housed 300 saddle- and draught horses and even the feeding troughs were made of marble. The beautiful **audience hall** on the first floor of the palace with a ceiling panel in which the Duke Waldstein himself is portrayed as the victor with the laurel wreath in a Roman triumphal carriage is worth seeing.

Towards the garden is the architectonically significant **Sala terrena** decorated with frescoes. In the spacious garden complex further on is a large birdhouse with peculiar stalactite imitations. The replica of the **bronze statues** (1622 to 1626) by Adrian de Fries

The only Gothic church originally built for the Benedictine monks was badly affected during the Hussite wars. Kilian Ignaz Dientzenhofer had the church remodelled in Baroque style in 1723–1731 and bestowed upon

St Thomas Church.

it the present appearance. The statue of St Augustine by Hieronymus Kohl can be seen over the main portal. Even the ceiling frescoes in the church's interior by Wenzel Lorenz Reiner show scenes from St Augustine's life. The pulpit and the main altar are attributed to Johann Anton Quittainer. The altar pieces are copies of the later works of Rubens.

The monastery was in the hands of the Augustine hermits since 1285. The order was awarded the right to brew in 1352 and Prague's oldest brewery was located here until 1953.

Kaunitz Palace 27
[Kounický palác, Mostecká 15, Praha 1]

The Baroque façades dominate in the lively Bridge Lane but it is not unusual that the foundations of the individual middle-class buildings and the palaces originate from the Middle Ages. The proud Kaunitz Palace built in the years 1773–1775 is comparatively young. The embassy of Serbia and Montenegro is located here today. The palace is adorned with stucco and sculptures from Ignaz Franz Platzer's workshop.

Schönborn Palace 28
[Schönbornský palác, Tržiště 15, Praha 1]

This palace serves as the American embassy and was built in the 17th century acquiring its present appearance around 1715.

The garden ascending towards Petřín Hill with a gloriette visible from afar is particularly splendid. Franz Kafka had a flat in the Schönborn Palace for a short period at the beginning of the 20th century.

Italian Lane 29
[Vlašská, Praha 1]

Among the artists and craftsmen in the court of Emperor Rudolph II were many Italian artists and craftsmen. They settled down in the Lesser Town at the foot of the Petřín Hill and built their own hospital and church since 1608.

In the second half of the 16th century the gardens in the area of the marketplace [Tržiště] and John's Hill [Jánský vršek] were divided into small plots intended to be built on. During that time emerged the Italian Lane [Vlašská] and Mountain Lane [Břetislavova]. There is obviously very little left today to sense the former Italian character of this part.

The **Hospital below the Petřín Hill** [Vlašská 36–40] is a double-

Italian Hospital in the Italian Lane.

Charles Borromeus Church.

storeyed four-winged structure that originally served as a convent and women's hospital. In 1851 the plain Charles Borromeus Church in empire style was built there too. The hospital is now a clinic of the Prague Faculty of Medicine.

The **Italian Hospital** [Vlašská 34] was a kind of charitable institution for the Italian community in Prague; the hospital church was built between 1608 and 1617. The institution was closed down under the rule of Joseph II; the Italians later turned it into an Italian orphanage in 1804. The cartouche next to the main portal of the church depicts the motif of the merciful Samaritan.

In the Second World War the so-called Casa d'Italia was set up in the premises of the Italian Hospital; the Italian Republic now maintains the Italian Cultural Institute here.

Lobkowicz Palace   **30**
[Lobkovický palác,
Vlašská 19, Praha 1]

This building was built in the place of a previous structure at the beginning of the 18th century; the high Baroque palace came into possession of the Bohemian noble family Lobkowicz in 1753. From its exterior facing the street, the Lobkowicz Palace seems cold and mighty but on the southern side it merges with the garden towards Petřín Hill. Czechoslovakia acquired this proud building in 1927 and used it for administrative purposes. The embassy of the People's Republic of China occupied it for a while. The diplomatic mission of the Federal Republic of Germany has been in the palace since 1973.

Lobkowicz Palace (garden view).

Lobkowicz Palace (from the castle ramp).

In autumn 1989 thousands of citizens of the GDR fled through the embassy of the FRG in Prague into the west. With that the Lobkowicz Palace became a place of German history in Prague. A car of the brand Trabant ironically placed on high legs by a Czech artist in the palace garden commemorates the mass flight. From the balcony on the south resting on columns, the (West) German Minister for Foreign Affairs at that time Hans-Dietrich Genscher announced to the jubilant refugees that nothing stood in the way of their exit into the Federal Republic anymore: "We have come here to inform you that it has been made possible for you to leave the country (GDR)." A commemorative plaque on the wall reminds us of this historical moment.

St Lawrence Church on the Petřín Hill.

Petřín Hill 31
[Petřín, Praha 1]

With a height of 322 m the Petřín Hill is a moderate height for day trips, an ascending hillock on the left embankment in the immediate neighbourhood of the Castle Hill; a funicular leaves from Újezd up to the hillock plateau, but to approach from the backside over the Italian Lane has its own charm too. On the crest of Petřín Hill are a few objects of interest – an observatory, a mirror maze [bludiště], the St Lawrence Church, beautiful rose gardens and a row of statues in honour of commendable personalities. In a pavilion

Observatory on the Petřín Hill.

The Mácha Monument on the Petřín Hill.

Observation tower
on the Petřín Hill.

Franz Kafka mentioned the Petřín Hill in his writings too (especially in the *Description of a Struggle*).

Church of Our Lady of Victory [32]
[Chrám Panny Marie Vítězné, Karmelitská 9, Praha 1]

The originally Protestant church of the Lesser Town Germans got its present name after the Battle of the White Mountain. This church was then handed over to the barefooted Carmelites followed by the order of St John of Jerusalem in 1784.

On a side-altar to the right is the gracious **Prague Infant Jesus**. The wax figure dressed in valuable robes originating from Spain in the 16th century is attributed with miraculous powers. A Spanish princess

one can see the panorama painting *The Battle against the Swedes on the Prague Bridge in 1648*. The biggest attraction on Petřín Hill is no doubt the 16 m high iron **observation tower** with its 299 steps to a breathtaking view. The Eiffel Tower was an apt model for this tower erected in 1891 and it reveals the admiration Prague felt for the grande nation and metropolis Paris towards the close of the 19th century.

Church of Our Lady of Victory.

Prague Infant Jesus.

13th century. This magnificent church was severely damaged in the Hussite wars in 1420 and a blazing fire in 1503 did the rest. Through the double portal under the characteristic Maltese cross one arrives in a kind of front garden and finally in the church's Baroque interior by Carlo Lurago. The Czech Baroque artist Karel Škréta contributed to the splendour. The altarpiece on the high altar (*The Assumption of the Holy Mary*) as well as the paintings *The Beheading of St Barbara* and *The Victory at Lepanto* are his work. Since 1857 a marble statue commemorates Grand Prior Count Rudolf Colleredo-Wallsee who led the heroic defence of Prague against the Swedes in 1648 and whose last resting-place is in front of the high altar.

brought it to Bohemia and her daughter, a princess Polyxena of Lobkowicz gifted it to the convent. In the pious Baroque times, the Prague Infant Jesus was honoured as miraculous. Since then the merciful site is visited by pilgrims from all over the world.

Maltese Church of St Mary below-the-chain
[Maltézský kostel „Panny Marie pod řetězem", Maltézské náměstí, Praha 1]

The Maltese Church of St Mary below-the-chain goes back to the 12th century with its fundaments when the order of St John of Jerusalem ran a hospital here. The three nave basilica belonging to this complex was built generously by the Maltese order in the

Nostitz Palace
[Nostický palác, Maltézské náměstí 1, Praha 1]

This impressive four-winged palace was built and splendidly decorated for the family Nostitz-Rieneck. From the early Baroque construction a lot reminds us of the progressive Renaissance period – but also later adjustments to the respective prevailing taste have left their traces, for example the statues of the Prague high Baroque sculptors Ferdinand Maximilian Brokoff and Matthias Bernhard Braun and the rococo decorations put up around 1770 and the portal by Anton Haffenecker as well as the ornamental empire style balconies on the second floor that were added in the 19th century. Nostitz Palace has a significant and valuable library consisting of about 14,000 volumes from the 17th century.

The Grand Priory Square

[Velkopřevorské náměstí, Praha 1]

The **Grand Priory building** [Velkopřevorské náměstí 4] stores the extensive archive of the Maltese – to be precise the order of the St John of Jerusalem the Grand Priory of which has been in the church since 1301.

The **Buquoy-Longueval Palace** [Velkopřevorské náměstí 2] was built in the second half of the 17th century at the orders of the Prague Archbishop Count Johann Friedrich of Waldstein. The French embassy is now located in this palace.

On the **John Lennon Wall**, the Czechs whose hearts throbbed for him especially in times of socialistic restrictions (and even more tourists) commemorate their great idol. Colourful graffiti paintings make the wall a living – but because it is painted over from time to time – also a transient work of art.

Kampa Island

[Ostrov Kampa, Praha 1]

Kampa Island, accessible from the Lesser Town (as well as from the Charles Bridge) lies between the River Vltava and the river arm "Devils Stream" [Čertovka]. Despite its location, the Kampa region came under the Old Town jurisdiction. Kampa Island was a storage place for trading commodities in the Middle Ages; in the course of the centuries, poor people, mostly washerwomen and raftsmen, settled down in this area that was subject to floods. Today Kampa Island is a tourism-oriented area with a smalltown character. It drifts over into a lively park in the southern part.

A particularly attractive part of Kampa Island is known as the "Venice of Prague" due to the buildings situated right by the water. A famous pottery market was held on the island for centuries.

House "At the Three Ostriches"

[Dům „U Tří pštrosů", Dražického náměstí 12, Praha 1]

The fresco adorned building on the Lesser Town end of the Charles Bridge originates from the closing years of the 16th century, the

Venice of Prague.

Row of houses on the Kampa Island (Na Kampě).

two gables were built on in the 17th century and are actually early Baroque. The first coffee house in Prague in about 1704, run by the Armenian immigrant Gorgos Hatalah el-Damaschi (Deodatus Damajan) from Damascus, was in this building.

St Joseph's Church   **38**
[Kostel sv. Josefa,
Josefská, Praha 1]

In the quiet Joseph Lane not far from the lively Bridge Lane we hit upon an estimable church. The foundation for the construction of this sacred building was laid in 1673 in the presence of Emperor Leopold I; the façade bears the Habsburg coat of arms even today. A considerable contribution to the structure with the elliptical ground plan was from the very important master builder and imperial court architect for Prague, Jean Baptiste

Mathey. The shell is supposed to have been ready about 1690 but the interior was worked on for more than a decade.

The church interior belongs both from the point of view of architecture as well as the furnishings and artistic arrangements amongst the most valuable in Prague. The main altar painting on the Baroque altar portrays the Holy Family and was painted by Peter Brandl in 1702. The picture of St Francis of Sales on top is the work of Josef Hellich (19th century). St Joseph's Church was meant as a church for the order of Carmelites Convent, the first female Carmel in Prague. About the end of the 18th century this convent came in to the hands of the order of English Virgins established by the Englishwoman Mary de Ward. The English Virgins tend to the church once again. Sunday mass is also held in English here.

Idyll on the Lesser Town bank of the Vltava.

Charles Bridge
[Karlův most]

The Charles Bridge made of stone.

On the Stone Bridge
[Karlův most]

Lesser Town Bridge Towers [39]
[Malostranské mostecké věže, Praha 1]

The smaller of the two towers originates from the same time as the Judith Bridge (second half of the 12th century), the first stone bridge built over the Vltava. The tower is considered among the oldest structures in this town (the roof and its ornaments however from the 16th century). The larger late Gothic tower was erected only in 1464. It was meant as a counterpart to the Old Town bridge towers.

On the late Gothic Lesser Town bridge towers, the heraldists cover their outlay: they can compare the former coat of arms of the Prague Old Town (three towers, city gate, semi-raised grille; the fist with the coat of arms holding a raised sword was only added after the Thirty Years' War) with the coat of arms of the Lesser Town (similarly three towers however with open gates and without a grille) here. The Gothic gate between the two towers was closed by nightfall in earlier centuries.

Towards the bridge before the smaller tower is the former customs office where the "Club for Old Prague" that contributes to the preservation of historic monuments has had a seat since 1901.

Charles Bridge [40]
[Karlův most, Praha 1]

The Gothic Charles Bridge is considered as one of the most important monuments of medieval architecture in Bohemia. As early as the 9th century there is believed to have been a ferry here that was, as the well-known Bohemian chronicler informs us, substituted by a wooden bridge by 1118. The first stone bridge replaced the wooden construction in 1158. This firmly established Judith Bridge served Prague

Lesser Town bridge towers, in front of it on the left, the former customs office.

residents for almost two centuries until it was swept away by the floods in 1342. At exactly the time predicted by the court astrologers – in the year 1357, on the 9th day of the 7th month, at 5:31 h – Emperor Charles IV laid the foundation for the construction of the new bridge that would stretch over the Vltava with sixteen arches and be about 5 m higher than its predecessor. The architect and master builder Peter Parler came from Schwäbisch Gmünd. The stone bridge remains the only connection between the Old Town of Prague and the Lesser Town until the 19th century.

Of the 30 **sculptures** on the Charles Bridge, mostly replaced by copies today, the one of St Nepomuk is the most important. It was cast in 1683 based on a model by Johann Brokoff in Nuremberg.

Old Town Bridge Tower

[Staroměstská mostecká věž, Praha 1]   **41**

With the construction of the Charles Bridge in 1357, Peter Parler also began building the Gothic defence tower on the Old Town bridgehead.

This tower was of great strategic significance in defending the Old Town (like against the Swedes in the Thirty Years' War). Fortunately this bulwark survived the violent centuries relatively undamaged. Only the ornamental figures on the west side were

Early morning on the Charles Bridge, the bronze statue of St Nepomuk to the left.

Charles Bridge at nighttime, Prague Castle and St Nicholas Church in the background.

destroyed and removed during the Swedish shooting raid in 1648. An old inscription commemorates it.

To the east of the tower, above the pointed archway, the coat of arms of countries that were reigned by Charles IV can be seen. Beneath the coat of arms is portrayed the kingfisher, symbol of King Wenceslas IV. Above the row of coat of arms stands St Vitus as the bridge protector on three bridge piers flanked by the two patrons: Charles IV (left) and Wenceslas IV (right). On the top floor of the tower are the saints Adalbert and Sigismund above the (Bohemian) lion sculpture inset in the façade.

One can climb up to the tower gallery through a spiral staircase and enjoy the view over the roof-tops of the Old Town. A small corridor leads into the cellar of the tower's formerly feared dungeon.

Old Town bridge tower (east side).

Statues on Prague's Charles Bridge
(Viewed from the Old Town Bridgehead)

LEFT PARAPET
(Looking from the Old Town towards the Lesser Town)

St Ivo, patron of advocates, made by Matthias Bernhard Braun in 1711.

SS Barbara, Margaret and Elizabeth made by Ferdinand Maximilian Brokoff in 1707.

Pietà, 1859 made by Emanuel Max. The last Swedish onslaught towards the end of the Thirty Years' War (1648) was parried from this spot with the help of students of Charles University (see panorama on Petřín Hill).

St Joseph made by Josef Max in 1854.

St Francis Xavier (the "Indian apostle") made by Ferdinand Maximilian Brokoff in 1711. The statue was badly damaged by the floods in 1890. The Jesuit father Francis Xavier (1506–1552) who did missionary work in countries including East India and Japan received his place on the bridge for the conversion of supposedly 1,2 million heathens whose varying origins are symbolised by the four kneeling figures.

St Christopher made by Emanuel Max in 1857. A marble plaque on the bridge tower mentions that the guardroom at this spot plunged into the waters along with the soldiers in the flood of 1784.

St Francis of Borgia, a Jesuit from Spain, made by Ferdinand Maximilian Brokoff in 1710.

RIGHT PARAPET
(Looking from the Old Town towards the Lesser Town)

St Bernard and the Holy Madonna made by Matthias Wenzel Jäckel in 1709.

SS Mary, Dominic and Thomas Aquinus made by Matthias Wenzel Jäckel in 1708.

Crucifix, 17th century. This bronze cross was cast by Hans Hillger in 1629 and was originally meant to adorn the Elbebridge in Dresden. In 1657 it was placed as the first sculpture on the Charles Bridge. The Hebrew inscription though was added only in 1696 with the money offered by a Jew who was fined for blasphemy of the Holy Cross.

The Virgin and Child with St Anne made by Matthias Wenzel Jäckel in 1707.

SS Cyril and Methodius with the three allegorical figures symbolising Bohemia, Moravia and Slovakia made by Karel Dvořák from 1628 to 1938. This most recent group of statues replaced the previous statue of St Ignatius Loyola.

St John the Baptist made by Josef Max in 1857. The marble plaque on the parapet signifies the place where John of Nepomuk was thrown into the Vltava in 1393 at the order of King Wenceslas IV.

SS Norbert, Sigismund and Wenceslas made by Josef Max in 1853.

St Ludmila, this statue of the first Christian duchess in the country was carved in about 1730 in Matthias Bernhard Braun's workshop and transferred here from the Church of the Virgin Mary's Retreat at the Castle Hill.

St Franciscus Seraphicus (better known as Francis of Assisi) made by Emanuel Max in 1855.

St Vincenz Ferrerius and Procopius made by Ferdinand Maximilian Brokoff in 1712. Below the parapet stands the Roland Column (also Bruncvík statue), a shield and sword bearing knight symbolising the City and Market Rights.

St Nicholas Tolentinus made by Johann Friedrich Kohl in 1708.

St Luitgard with the Crucified made by Matthias Bernhard Braun in 1710 based on a sketch by Peter Brandl.

St Adalbert, national patron saint and Bishop of Prague, made by Michael Josef Brokoff in 1709.

SS John of Matha, Ivan, Felix of Valois with the Turkish guards watching over the Christian slaves made by Ferdinand Maximilian Brokoff in 1714. John of Matha and Felix of Valois were the founders of the order of Trinity which was established in 1198 to buy freedom for the Christian captives. St Ivan as opposed to them – easy to recognise by the full beard and long hair – is considered to be the first Bohemian hermit.

St Wenceslas, Bohemian national patron saint made by Josef Kamil Böhm in 1858. The Bohemian duke Wenceslas (about 903–929) a grandson of St Ludmila worked intensively towards Christianising the country and Bohemia's integration into the Holy Roman Empire. Due to this he came into conflict with the heathen national reactions under the leadership of his brother Boleslav I who had him assassinated. The death anniversary of St Wenceslas (28th September) is an official holiday.

St John of Nepomuk, Vicar General of the Archbishopric of Prague. Bronze statue based on the models of Johann Brokoff and Matthias Rauchmüller cast by Wolfgang Hieronymus Heroldt in Nuremberg. John of Nepomuk is considered the martyr of the seal of confession because he is said to have refused to divulge to King Wenceslas IV the latter's wife's confession.

St Antonius of Padua made by Johann Ulrich Mayer in 1707, a sculptor presumably from Vienna who possessed civil rights in the Lesser Town of Prague since 1712.

St Judas Thaddeus, apostle, by Johann Ulrich Mayer in 1708.

St Augustine, church teacher by Johann Friedrich Kohl in 1708.

St Kajetan with angels, by Ferdinand Maximilian Brokoff in 1709.

St Philip Benitius by Michael Bernhard Mändl around 1711. The area beneath the statue is known as the "Venice of Prague".

St Vitus on a cliff with lions, patron saint of the Prague Bridge by Ferdinand Maximilian Brokoff in 1714.

SS Cosmas and Damian patron saint of physicians and apothecaries by Johann Ulrich Mayer in 1709.

The Virgin and Child with St Anne.

The Old Town
[Staré Město]

A Walk through the Old Town
[Staré Město]

Embedded in the riverbend, with the river flowing around it in a semicircle and therefore ideally protected, is the location of the first of the four historical cities of Prague: the Old Town of Prague. Its beginnings go back to the first century of the Christian calendar – there was obviously no reason to name the small market town Old Town at that time. This term came to be used only after Charles IV founded the "New Town" in the 14th century. The Prague Jewish Town developed in the northwest of the Old Town area bordering directly on the banks of the River Vltava. The centre of the Old Town consists of the Old Town Square with its dominant City Hall and Týn Church. Another significant city-core developed around the St Gallus Church [kostel sv. Havla]: the Gallus Town.

In the course of the administrative reform under Emperor Joseph II, the Prague towns – namely Castle District, the Lesser Town, New Town and Old Town – united in 1784. From then onwards, the City Hall of Prague was located at the Old Town Square.

In the 20th century the Old Town of Prague underwent some drastic changes that have robbed the area of a lot of its former charm. The redevelopment of the Prague Jewish Quarter (about 1900) can be cited as an example, the politically driven removal of the Marian column that used to be in front of the City Hall (1918) and the destruction of the east wing

Proud middle-class buildings to the north of Old Town Square.

of the neo-Gothic City Hall during the Prague rebellions in May 1945. Despite many losses the Old Town of Prague is counted amongst the most beautiful historical ensembles of Europe today.

Old Town Square

[Staroměstské náměstí, Praha 1]

If Wenceslas Square in the New Town is the culmination point in the recent national history so the walls of the Old Town Square mirror the happenings of past centuries that have found expression in significant buildings. The square is laid out, not square or rectangular, but displays an extremely irregular turbulent ground plan. Romanesque, Gothic, Renaissance and Baroque united into a unique composition that is rightly perceived as the centre of the historical city of Prague. The important monuments, palaces and churches are joined by proud middle-class buildings with an individual history going back into the Middle Ages.

"**At the Minute**" [Staroměstské náměstí 2] is where the writer Franz Kafka's family lived between July 1889 and September 1896. Kafka's three sisters Elli, Valli and Ottla were born here. This building has a (though painted over in Kafka's time) sgraffito façade from the beginning of the 17th century. The guarding lion on the building corner is the trademark of the former pharmacy "**At the White Lion**" situated here.

In the house "**At the Golden Angels**" [Staroměstské náměstí 29] is the famous restaurant "**At the Prince**" where the German poet Detlev von Liliencron made a stop during his visit to Prague. The St Florian sculpture originates from the 18th century.

House "At the Minute", one of the Kafka places in Prague.

In the house "**At the Blue Goose**" [Staroměstské náměstí 25] was the trusser wine and beer house where the German painter Carl Spitzweg tippled in 1849.

In the house "**At the Golden Unicorn**" [Staroměstské náměstí 20] was the residence of the Czech poet Karel Havlíček Borovský in the years 1838 /39. Later on Bedřich Smetana had a music school here.

In the house "**At the Unicorn Pharmacy**" [Staroměstské náměstí 17] the apothecary's wife Berta Fanta had a literary salon frequented by personalities like Franz Kafka, Max Brod and Albert Einstein.

The "**Štorch House**" [Staroměstské náměstí 16] in the Vladislavistic Gothic style is known through its painted façade designed by the Czech painter Mikoláš Aleš (*Portrayal of St Wenceslas*). The name of the building commemorates the builder and architect, the Prague publisher Alexander Štorch.

The "**Oppelt House**" [Staroměstské náměstí 3] was one of Franz Kafka's homes. Including others he wrote the narrations *The Verdict* and *The Metamorphosis* here.

Old Town City Hall 43
[Staroměstská radnice,
Staroměstské náměstí 3, Praha 1]

After King John of Luxembourg had sanctioned the construction of the City Hall in 1338, the citizens of the Old Town of Prague enabled through wine taxes the purchase of a private building on the Old Town Square. A council chamber was furnished, and a flat for the town clerk and cells for captives. The Gothic City Hall tower was built in 1364, the first of its kind in medieval Prague. During the rule of Wenceslas IV, the St Andreas Chapel on the second floor was consecrated in 1381. The original City Hall was destroyed in a fire in 1399 and was rebuilt in 1407. A remarkable change was brought on by the elegant development of the neo-Gothic north wing in the 19th century.

During the violent confrontations in May 1945 the neo-Gothic north wing and the east wing of the Prague City Hall were destroyed. Fortunately the tower remained intact. The famous Apostle (Astronomical) Clock originating from 1410 could be restarted after the Second World War.

The Apostle Clock is a mirror of the medieval view of the world: The planets are depicted circling the earth not the sun. The hour hand moves ahead a day at the stroke of midnight. The saviour and 12 apostle figures carved out of wood show themselves at the hour. When all the disciples have passed by a golden cockerel crows in the tympanum. Beneath it to the right, death sways its hourglass and rings the death knell. On the left, the man standing next to the dial cannot buy himself free from his fate despite his

The tower of the Old Town City Hall.

The Astronomical Clock at the City Hall.

Renaissance window on the façade of the Old Town City Hall.

bulging moneybag; death shakes his head at such desperate bribery attempts. Vanity is portrayed allegorically, miserliness and heathenism too. Archangel Michael warns with shield and sword of the Last Judgement. In 1866, the art clock [Czech: orloj from "Horologium"] was replaced by the plate with medallions for the twelve months of the year (painted by Josef Mánes).

Adjacent to the Astronomical Clock, a late Gothic portal leads inside the City Hall. On the second floor is the late Gothic **council chamber** with a painted ceiling with wooden beams from

the Renaissance period, a coat of arms of the city, a cross and several dozen signs of guilds. A new **meeting hall** was built in 1879. It bears impressive historical paintings by Václav Brožík: *Election of George of Poděbrady as King of Bohemia* (took place in 1458 in the Old Town City Hall) and *Jan Hus before the Council of Constance*. The freely accessible **vestibule** with mosaic pictures based on works of the Czech painter Mikoláš Aleš (including: *Libuše predicts Prague's fame*) is worth seeing.

Also belonging to the City Hall, is the adjoining Renaissance tract on the left, with an extraordinarily beautiful window made in three parts bearing the inscription PRAGA CAPUT REGNI as well as the Prague City coat of arms.

The old Town Hall now serves only representational purposes. The most popular wedding hall in the country is in this building.

Since the Middle Ages, the pillory and the place of execution were placed in front of the Town Hall. Included in every Czech school history book is an execution that took place here on 21ˢᵗ June 1621: 27 Protestant rebels (Germans and Czechs) including the Rector of Charles University, Dr. med. Johann Jesenius, were executed at the scaffold beneath the bay chapel. 27 crosses on the pavement in front of the City Hall reminded people of this expiation after the Battle of the White Mountain.

St Nicholas Church in the Old Town.

St Nicholas Church in the Old Town `44`

[Kostel sv. Mikuláše na Starém Městě, Staroměstské náměstí, Praha 1]

This splendid Baroque St Nicholas Church was built in 1732–1737 in the immediate neighbourhood of the (former) Jewish Quarter. It is the work of the great Kilian Ignaz Dientzenhofer.

The figures adorning the exterior are by Anton Braun, Matthias Bernhard Braun's nephew. The founders of the order, Benedict and Norbert flank the portals to the south of the church, in the recesses are the holy physicians Cosmas and Damian.

In the church interior is an admirably splendid chandelier from the bohemian town in the Giant Mountains, Harrachov, and a large fresco in the octagonal dome with a legend of St Nicholas as the theme. In the course of the Josephine Reforms in 1787 this church was profaned and made into a warehouse. About a century later in 1874 the church was utilised for Russian-Orthodox mass. After the First World War the St Nicholas Church in the Old Town became the main church of the Czechoslovakian Hussite Church.

Kinsky Palace `45`

[Palác Kinských, Staroměstské náměstí 12, Praha 1]

This proud Baroque building is a mature later work of Kilian Ignaz Dientzenhofer carried out by

Kinsky Palace (left) and the house „At the Stone Bell" (right).

Anselmo Lurago (1755–1765). The sculptural decorations on the palace attica came from Ignaz Franz Platzer's workshop. The empire style stairwell from the years 1835–1836 is noteworthy. The palace, initially built for Johann Arnold of Goltz, came into the ownership of the Kinsky family in 1786 that were then expropriated of it after the Second World War as a result of the Beneš decrees. Today this building on the Old Town Square striking from afar with its unique rococo façade belongs to the National Gallery. Bertha von Suttner (*Lay Down Your Arms*, 1905), Nobel Peace Prize winner, born in 1843 spent the early years of her childhood in the Kinsky Palace.

From September 1893 Franz Kafka went to the German-speaking humanist state grammar school that was situated in the courtyard.

He was to eventually take the school leaving examination at this institution in September 1901. Later on Kafka's father's haberdashery shop was also in the same building. A bookshop occupies these rooms today thus commemorating the great Prague author.

On 21ˢᵗ February 1948 the communist Prime Minister Klement Gottwald announced from the balcony of the Kinsky Palace, the resignation of the non-socialist minister; successively Czechoslovakia became a communist nation.

House "At the Stone Bell" 46

[Dům „U Kamenného zvonu",
Staroměstské náměstí 13, Praha 1]

This three-storeyed tower building was built on the foundations of an early Gothic residential

119

building in the second half of 13th century. In the process of a second construction period about 1310, the chapel was made with rich figures and ornamental adornments of which unfortunately only fragments exist now. The characteristic house symbol on the house corner, the stone bell was installed in the 16th century. Alterations after 1685 as well as in the 18th and 19th century strongly changed the appearance of the building. After extensive research and reconstruction works, the building reattained more or less its original late medieval appearance in the 1980s. Presently the hall in the house "At the Stone Bell" is used for concerts and exhibitions.

Church of Our Lady before Týn   **47**
[Chrám Matky Boží před Týnem, Staroměstské náměstí, Praha 1]

"Our Lady before Týn" was founded by traders and merchants in the mid 14th century. The construction work was done by Peter Parler's cathedral stonemasonry. The 80 m high towers with eight pointed spires each is a characteristic landmark in the maze of roofs in the Old Town.

The arcade – like porch that restricts the view of the church housed the famous "Týn School" even in the Middle Ages.

The construction was stopped during the Hussite unrest. The elected King George of Poděbrady had the church and the two distinctive towers on it com-

pleted. This was the main church of the Hussites between 1419 and 1621. A statue of George of Poděbrady with a drawn sword portrayed as the protector of the Hussite chalice was placed on the gable roof. It was removed soon after the victory of the Catholic Habsburgs at the Battle of the White Mountain and the gilded chalice was thereafter melted into the halo for the predominant Madonna statue on the gable roof.

In the church interior is the marble tomb of the important Danish astronomer Tycho de Brahe. Emperor Rudolph II summoned him to Prague in 1599. The life-size relief figure is dressed in full armour.

In addition there are several panels by the Czech Baroque painter Karel Škréta (for example, *The Angelic Salutation* on the proclamation altar or *The Assumption* on the high altar) in

Towers of the Týn Church.

the church. To the pièce de résistance of the lavish decor belongs: a statue of the Slavic apostles Cyril and Methodius made of Carrara marble, a large wooden crucifix from the times of Charles IV, a late Gothic stone baldachin by Matthias Rejsek over the grave of the Italian suffragan bishop Augustinus Lucianus of Mirandola, a Gothic pulpit from the 15th century, a carved altar with a portrayal of the Baptism of Christ, a pewter font in the shape of an upside-down bell bearing an Apostle relief, the Lady before Týn made from limetree wood and a high Baroque oval relief of the Holy Family (beneath the organ loft).

Prague author Franz Kafka.

Birthplace of the Author Franz Kafka
[náměstí Franze Kafky 5, Praha 1] **49**

Franz Kafka was born on 3rd July 1883 as the first of six children of the haberdashery shopholder Hermann Kafka and his wife Julie. The building he was born in, situated to the north of Old Town Square, was in those days on the border of the still existent Prague ghetto, in the immediate neighbourhood of St Nicholas Church. This building was built between 1717 and 1730 by Kilian Ignaz Dientzenhofer as the "Prelature to St Nicholas in the Old Town". After the rescindment of the monastery in 1787 under Emperor Joseph II it was converted into a residential building.

In place of the building that was burned down in 1897 a tenement block was erected; only the portal of the original house remained.

Jan Hus monument.

Jan Hus Monument
[Pomník Jana Husa, Staroměstské náměstí, Praha 1] **48**

This monument by Ladislav Šaloun, too large as compared to the extent of the square, was unveiled on 6 July 1915 on the 500th anniversary of the reformer Jan Hus' burning to death. The upright Hus looks at the Týn Church that was the Hussite Bishop's Church for a while.

Franz Kafka's birthplace.

There is a small Kafka exhibition in the building now. In 1965, a commemorative bust was placed on the exterior of the building. Seventy-six years after the death of evidently the most famous son of the city, the square in front of his birthplace has been renamed Franz Kafka Square.

Celetná Lane

[Celetná, Praha 1]

50

The promenade and shopping lane leading from Old Town Square to Republic Square belongs to the so-called "Royal Path". The participants of the ceremonial coronation procession from the Royal Palace in the Old Town to the St Vitus Cathedral which was the coronation church traipsed along this route. During unsafe times, the Bohemian kings returned to the fortified Prague Castle and the Royal Path lost its meaning.

Illustrious personalities like Cola da Rienzi, Francesco Petrarca or Johannes Faust were guests in the **"Sixt House"** [Celetná 2]. In the 17th century it belonged to the secretary Phillipus Fabricius who was thrown out of the old chancellery in 1618. He survived the Defenestration and was consequently titled "von Hohenfall" (of the high fall). The child Franz Kafka also lived in this building in 1888/89.

In the house **"At the Three Kings"** [Celetná 3] Kafka lived in his youth.

The house **"At the White Lion"** [Celetná 6] is adorned with an original house symbol.

Mozart's hostess in Prague, the pharmacist's daughter Josepha Dušková used to live in the house **"At the Black Sun"** [Celetná 8].

The house **"At the White Peacock"** [Celetná 10] impresses with its rococo façade and an original house symbol.

Hermann Kafka's shop was in the **Hrzán of Harasov Palace** [Celetná 12] for a while. The palace was presumably built based on the plans made by Giovanni Alliprandi.

The **Caretto-Millesimo Palace** [Celetná 13] is a palace rebuilt in the Baroque style on a Romanesque foundation with an especially beautiful Baroque portal.

The **Buquoy Palace** [Celetná 20] has a beautiful Renaissance portal.

Celetná Lane.

House symbol "At the Golden Angel".

The house **"At the Vulture"** [Celetná 22] used to be a brewery. It has been an auditorium of the Charles University since the 18th century. Over the Baroque portal is a gold inscription reminding of the formerly established "Imperial and Royal Gold Articles factory of Prokop Hindle & son". Since 1861 the building housed Mercy Printers, the main office of the famous *Prager Tagblatt* and the editorial department of the *Prager Morgenpost*.

The **"Manhart House"** [Celetná 17] used to be a Piarist College; a Baroque Nepomuk statue is prominently displayed on the façade above the first storey.

The house **"At the Red Eagle"** [Celetná 21] demonstrates a particularly beautiful house symbol.

The house **"At the Bohemian Eagle"** [Celetná 30] is a block of rented flats from 1897 in the Czech neo-Renaissance style.

The house **"At the Black Madonna"** [Celetná 34] was built by Josef Gočár in 1911/12. It was the first cubist building in Europe.

The house **"At the Four Columns"** [Celetná 25] in the home and place of death of the philosopher and the theologist Bernard Bolzano.

In place of the house **"At the Temple"** [Celetná 27] there formerly were a church and a hospital.

The house **"At the Golden Angel"** [Celetná 29] used to be a hotel where in 1848 the revolutionary Mikhail Bakunin and later on also the German author Theodor Fontane, working as a war reporter, were accommodated.

The **Pachta Palace** [Celetná 36] was originally a mint and since 1784, the Prague military Commandant's headquarters. During the Prague Whitsun uprising in 1848, the first shooting between the revolutionaries and troops of the Prague military Commandant General Windischgrätz took place in front of this building. Since 1850 it serves as a court building, even Franz Kafka worked here. The sculptural building adornment comes from Ignaz Franz Platzer.

Powder Tower   51
[Prašná brána, Celetná, Praha 1]

In place of the dilapidated state of the Kutná Hora Gate from the 13th century through which the street led to the silver city Kutná Hora, a 65 m high tower was erected in 1475. The rector of the Týn School, Master Matthias Rejsek was responsible for its construction. It bears the name

The Gothic Powder Tower.

because it was occasionally used to store gunpowder. It was connected to the neighbouring royal court by a wooden bridge. The tower was badly damaged by the Prussian artillery shooting in 1757. The tower was completed by cathedral master builder Josef Mocker in a neo-Gothic style in the 19th century.

Two lavishly adorned halls can be viewed in the interior of the Powder Tower.

Municipal House `52`
[Obecní dům,
náměstí Republiky 5, Praha 1]

The representative Municipal House in the so-called Prague Secession style was built in the years 1906 to 1912 in place of the former royal court. The "Repre" as the Prague folk call it, is the known venue for representative balls, concerts (especially in Smetana Hall) and meetings. There is a tradition-laden café and an elegant restaurant on the ground floor.

The architects Osvald Polívka and Antonín Balšánek tried to emphasise a national romantic note (for example, relief medallions depicting traditional costumes). A mosaic by Karel Špillar portrays a *Homage to Prague*. Ladislav Šaloun contributed beautiful groups of statues too, they symbolise the humiliation and the resurrection of the people. The Secession artist Alfons Mucha created valuable allegorical paintings in the "Mayor's Hall". The Czechoslovakian Republic was proclaimed in the representation house on 28 October 1918, in 1989 a round table at which the then communist leadership negotiated with the opposition under the chairmanship of Václav Havel was held here.

Mosaic on Obecní dům: Libuše predicts fame for Prague.

St Jacobs Church [53]

[Kostel sv. Jakuba,
Malá Štupartská, Praha 1]

This church is decorated on the outside with the stucco reliefs (1695) by Ottavio Mosto with the church of the Minorite monastery founded by Wenceslas I. The monastery buildings are only partly preserved.

The three nave basilica was completed in 1374. Its Baroque decor is from the first half of the 18th century. The altarpiece on the high altar from 1739 depicts the death of the martyr St Jacobs and is the work of the Bohemian Baroque painter Wenzel Lorenz Reiner. In the side hall is an almost 9 m high tomb by Johann Bernhard Fischer von Erlach and Ferdinand Maximilian Brokoff erected for the Bohemian Chancellor Count Johann Wenzel Vratislav of Mitrowicz (died 1712).

Due to its good organ and excellent acoustics, concerts and musical high masses are organised in this church. The Czech organist Bohuslav Czernohorský performed on this church organ.

Týn Courtyard ["Ungelt"] [54]

[Týnský dvůr, Praha 1]

The main building of the courtyard complex better known as Týn Courtyard is the building where the legendary tax collector Jakob of Granov had his seat. This Renaissance palace with an open loggia on the first floor (wall panels and sgraffitos from the 16th century with biblical and mythological themes) served as quarters for foreign traders. Over the portal are inscribed the Granov family's coat of arms and the year 1560. The complex was burned down in the 17th century; ordinary houses were built in the place of the old customs court. The German term "Ungelt" (also used for this courtyard) reminds us of the medieval function of the ducal customs court. Traders travelling through were expected to pay storage and customs charges for all the wares that would pass through Bohemia in this building. Foreign traders were only permitted to transship wares through the obviously not commission free office of the local official in the Týn Courtyard.

In the Týn Courtyard ("Ungelt").

Carolinum `55`
[Karolinum,
Železná/Ovocný trh, Praha 1]

The famous Charles University, founded by the Emperor Charles IV on 7 April 1348 as the first university north of the Alps, was moved in 1383 to the house of the royal coin maker Johann Rotlöw on the spot of the present day Carolinum quarter.

Carolinum's Gothic oriel window.

Only a magnificent Gothic oriel window – part of the SS Cosmas and Damian Chapel (about 1370) – an archway and the hall on the second floor where academic ceremonies take place even today remind us of the beginning of this great school. Charles University is, since its early days, also a mirror of the Bohemian national history.

After a short blossom period at the beginning of the 15ᵗʰ century, with the Kuttenberg Decree in 1409 when King Wenceslas IV gave in to the demand of rector Jan Hus for a majority of Bohemian nations in the university self-administration, came the downfall of the university.

The "natio bohemica" which included German and Czech citizens from Bohemian crownlands now had three votes as opposed to the Bavarian, Saxon and Polish university nations who had to be content with just one vote. Thereupon a great number of students, university teachers and professors left Charles University for other universities (Krakow, Heidelberg, Vienna, Cologne; in fact a new university was founded in Leipzig). Until the Jesuits took over in 1622 Charles University had the reputation of a heretic's nest in the Christian world.

Even in the 19ᵗʰ and 20ᵗʰ century, the great school was the scene of national and political clashes. In 1882 the university was divided into an independent Czech and a German University. The Czech University was closed down on 17ᵗʰ November 1939 at the orders of the Reich Protector, President Edvard Beneš avenged this with a repercussive closing down of the German University in

1945. Charles University was meant to play a significant part two more times in the political history of the land: during the months of the so-called Prague Spring in 1967/68 and in 1989 when the students body played a vital role in the "Velvet Revolution" exactly 50 years since the closure of the Czech University by the NS authorities.

Estates Theatre 56
[Stavovské divadlo, Ovocný trh 1, Praha 1]

This classicist theatre was originally named Nostitz Theatre after its builder Count Franz Anton Nostitz-Rieneck. It was built between 1781 and 1783 in close proximity to the Charles University – much to the regret of the professoriate who feared the student's distraction from their studies due to the theatre. The

Estates Theatre in the Old Town.

premiere of important operas were held in the Estates Theatre, for example Mozart's *Don Giovanni* (1787) and *La clemenza di Tito* (1791). Famous artists like Niccolò Paganini, Clara Schumann, Richard Wagner or Carl Maria von Weber performed here frequently.

The theatre served as the backdrop for director Miloš Forman's Mozart film *Amadeus* shortly before the building was closed down due to pending renovations in 1983.

St Gallus Church 57
[Kostel sv. Havla, Havelská, Praha 1]

The church with the beautifully curved Baroque façade and the area with the same name owe their names to the skull relic of St Gallus bought in the Middle Ages in St Gallen, Switzerland. Innumerable pilgrims came to Prague to view the relic – until it was lost during the Hussite wars. Important theologists and preachers worked in the St Gallus Church, including Jan Hus and John of Nepomuk.

Karel Škréta, one of the most significant Czech Baroque painters in the country, found his last resting-place here.

The church's surroundings, known as Gallus Town, is a part of Prague going back into the Middle Ages. In the charming Gallus Lane [Havelská], Gothic arcades still remind us of the epoch in which a large number of the German citizens settled here. The stalls of the street market situated here since 1232 give a feeling of the atmosphere of a medieval market place even today.

House "At the Two Golden Bears" 58

[Dům „U Dvou zlatých medvědů“, Kožná 1, Praha 1]

At the junction of the Leather Lane [Kožná ulička] and the Melantrichova Lane is the building that is particularly conspicuous through its Renaissance portal and its house symbol (two bears). It is the birthplace of the "Racing Reporter", Egon Erwin Kisch (1885–1948). Kisch belongs next to Franz Kafka, Max Brod, Rainer Maria Rilke and Franz Werfel to the German-speaking Prague writers famous beyond the country's borders.

Coal Market 59

[Uhelný trh, Praha 1]

There is a charming empire fountain from the year 1797 with figures made by Franz Xaver Lederer at the coal market. The Prague folk also call it the Wimmer fountain after its donor. The name of the area is derived from an old smithy with a charcoal kiln that was situated here until the early 19th century. This smithy, as the rumour goes, was one of Faust's lodgings in Prague.

Wolfgang Amadeus Mozart lived in the house "At the Three Lions" [Uhelný trh 1] in 1787

so that the musical director could be close to the Estates Theatre for the rehearsals of his opera *Don Giovanni*.

The house "At the Cancasters" [Uhelný trh 6] is the former editorial department of the *Prager Postzeitung*.

The house "At the Two Cats" [Uhelný trh 10] is a well-known Pilsner beer restaurant. There used to be a famous piano shop in this building in the 19th century; Antonín Dvořák performed in front of an audience for the first time in these rooms.

The Hungarian composer Franz Liszt lived in "Platýz" [Uhelný trh 11] between 1840 and 1846. As Prague's first block of rented flats it yielded considerable returns and the building was hence renamed "At the Golden Hen".

Church of "St Martin in the Wall" 60

[Kostel sv. Martina ve zdi, Martinská 8, Praha 1]

On the former city walls is a Gothic parish church "St Martin in the Wall" that now serves the Evangelical Bohemian Brethren Congregation. The Bohemian Baroque sculptor Ferdinand Maximilian Brokoff (1688–1731) and his family are buried in the St Martin's Cemetery that formally belonged to the church. This church earned significance in the history of the Hussite movement as the first to give communion in both forms (bread and wine) to believers "sub utraque specie" in 1414. As ultimately the opinions on wine differed, the chalice became the symbol of the Hussite revolution. The Utraquists read mass in Czech until the Counter-Reformation – even this was one of the main demands of the Hussite reformers.

Bethlehem Chapel 61
[Betlémská kaple,
Betlémské náměstí, Praha 1]

In this chapel founded in 1391, the rector of the Prague University Master Jan Hus headed fiery speeches since 1402 against the serious shortcomings and decline of moral standards in the church. The Bethlehem Chapel is a monument of great symbolic significance for this reason. The German reformer Thomas Müntzer preached here in 1521. After the Thirty Years' War the Jesuits were summoned to Prague to revive Catholicism tried to also remove the Bethlehem Chapel by reviving memories of the wretched "heresy". This national shrine was finally demolished in 1786. In the 1950s the Bethlehem Chapel was built anew on the remains of the walls of the historical chapel.

Little Square 62
[Malé náměstí, Praha 1]

This idyllic square was the area of Prague pharmacies in earlier centuries. In the centre of the square is a beautiful fountain arched over by an artistic wrought-iron grille from the 16th century.

Bethlehem Chapel
on Bethlehem Square.

Bohemian fountain lion
at the Little Square.

Since 1650 a gilded Bohemian lion adorns the top of the fountain grille.

The **Judge's Building** [Malé náměstí 11] was the oldest pharmacy in Prague.

The house **"At the Golden Lily"** [Malé náměstí 12] is also a former pharmacy.

The house **"At the Golden Crown"** [Malé náměstí 13] is a pharmacy even today. The architect and master builder Christoph Dientzenhofer lived here about 1700 AD.

Angelus of Florence, the court pharmacist of Charles IV worked in the house **"At the Angel"** [Malé náměstí 1].

The house **"At the White Lion"** [Malé náměstí 2] has a Gothic portal with a lion coat of arms on the spandrel as well as the rococo relief with the resurrection of Christ.

The **Rott House** [Malé náměstí 3] impresses with its historic wall paintings based on the sketches of Mikoláš Aleš. The first Bible in Czech was printed in this building.

Marian Square [63]
[Mariánské náměstí, Praha 1]

The special architectonic charm of the Marian Square is often overlooked by hurried visitors because the modern city square is surrounded by dominating palatial buildings. A lovable detail next to the towering palaces is the fountain statue of the Vltava on the garden wall of the Clam-Gallas Palace. The allegory is a creation of the most important representative of Prague classicism Wenzel Prachner (1812) and is tenderly called "Terezka" in the vernacular.

The **Prague City Library** [Mariánské náměstí 1] is a palace from the 1920s built by František Roith in the style of representative functionalism. The representation flat of the Mayor of Prague is in this building. A puppet theatre once found a home in this building too.

Middle-class buildings at the Little Square.

New City Hall at the Marian Square.

The **New City Hall** [Mariánské náměstí 2], a splendid art nouveau building, is the official residence of the Mayor of Prague. The two legendary figures integrated in the building's corners *The Black Knight* and *Rabbi Loew* by Ladislav Šaloun are really striking.

Clam-Gallas Palace 64

[Clam-Gallasův palác, Husova 20, Praha 1]

The Clam-Gallas Palace is one of the masterpieces of Baroque architecture in Prague, teamwork of excellent contemporary architects, sculptors and painters resulting in harmonic ensembles of secular architecture. The imperial court architect in Vienna, Johann Bernhard Fischer von Erlach, personally drew up the plans in 1713, an Italian – Domenico Canevale –was responsible for the construction. Matthias Bernhard Braun contributed the two Giant pairs that guard the portals. A ceiling fresco in the obviously most beautiful stairwell in the city worthy

4

Rabbi Loew at the New City Hall.

Façade of the Clam-Gallas Palace.

Staircase of the Clam-Gallas Palace.

of admiration is the *Triumph of Apollo* by Carlo Carlone.

The Clam-Gallas Palace was a manor-house for the Country Marshall of Bohemia, Johann Wenceslaus Count of Gallas who after a diplomatic career succeeded in becoming the Viceroy of Naples. The Prague City Archive

Telamones at the portal to Clam-Gallas Palace.

administers a rich stock of views, engravings, old maps, photographs, certificates, signets etc.

Dominican Church of St Aegidius 65
[Dominikánský kostel sv. Jiljí, Jilská, Praha 1]

This hall church built before 1370 without a choir loft but with equally high middle and side knaves takes a special place within the sacral architecture in Prague. St Aegidius Church was the victim of a great fire and had to be rebuilt as a result. The Dominicans took over this church in 1626 and had the early Baroque monastery complex built on by Carlo Lurago. The church's interior was remodelled to Baroque henceforth. The plans were presumably delivered by Kilian Ignaz Dientzenhofer.

Wenzel Lorenz Reiner (1689–1743), Bohemia's most important Baroque painter is buried in the side nave to the right in this Dominican church. Reiner is also the creator of many of the frescoes in the church interior (central nave: *Triumph of the Dominicans over the heretics*, side nave: *St Wenceslas*). The main altarpiece by Friedrich Johann Hess depicts the founding of the order of the Dominicans. The country's first music conservatoire was located here in the 19th century.

Rotunda of the Holy Cross 66
[Rotunda sv. Kříže, Karoliny Světlé, Praha 1]

This Romanesque round chapel of the Holy Cross was built at the beginning of the 12th century. It was closed down in 1784. Thanks to the initiative of a group of artists, the Romanesque gem was not torn down in the 19th century. The rotunda was restored in those days whereby Gothic wall panels from the 14th century were uncovered.

The iron grille around the chapel was designed by the Czech painter Josef Mánes.

Smetana Museum on Novotný footbridge 67
[Smetanovo muzeum, Novotného lávka 2, Praha 1]

Rotunda of the Holy Cross.

This neo-Renaissance building from 1885 served as the office of the Municipal Waterworks Department in the 1930s. Since Bedřich Smetana had lived in the nearby Lažanský-Palace on the Vltava embankment from 1868 to 1869 and composed his famous opera *The Bartered Bride*, a museum for the Czech composer was set up in the former building of the Prague Waterworks on Novotný footbridge.

The maestro's manuscripts and exhibits from his personal effects are displayed here. A monument for the composer stands in front of the Smetana Museum since 1984.

Novotný footbridge on the Old Town embankment, Smetana Museum to the left.

Knights of the Cross Square.

Knights of the Cross Square

68

[Křižovnické náměstí, Praha 1]

The Old Town bridge tower is one of the most beautiful bridge towers in Europe, the statue of Emperor Charles IV, St Salvator Church with the Clementinum and the Church of the Order of the Knights of the Cross and with that the marvellous view of the River Vltava and the Prague Castle as well as the Lesser Town and the Old Town towers – all this makes **the Knights of the Cross Square** one of the magnificent squares in Prague. The Prague folk also refer to it as their "Salon", a lovable description that does not bring to mind any of the thundering traffic and masses of tourists.

A statue of Emperor Charles IV dominates the square. Charles displays the

foundation certificate of the Prague University founded by him; with it are allegories of the former historical faculties as well as significant fellow-men of the Luxembourgs, amongst them Matthew of Arras, the first master builder of the St Vitus Cathedral. This monument cast in Nuremberg was supposed to be installed on the occasion of the 500th Jubilee of the Charles University but due to revolutionary turmoil in 1848, this plan could only be implemented in 1849.

At the corner of the Church of the Order of the Knights of the Cross, towards the street is a Baroque winegrower's column made by Johann Georg Bendl. The Prague City Council commissioned the statue of St Wenceslas on a column entwined with vine leaves in 1676. It originally stood at the winegrower's office at the end of the Charles Bridge. It had to be transferred here for traffic reasons. The medieval road surface of the street leading to the Judith Bridge in the 13th century can still be seen

Statue of Charles IV.

around the winegrower's column. It was uncovered by canal builders in 1910 and preserved for posterity.

Church of the Order of the Knights of the Cross St Franciscus Seraphicus
[Kostel sv. Františka Serafínského, Křižovnické náměstí, Praha 1]

The monastery church of the greatly esteemed and the sole one of the order of the knights founded in Bohemia, the "Knights of the Cross with a Red Star" is a replica of St Peter's Cathedral in Rome and like its model impresses first and foremost with its magnificent dome. The church façade with angel figures and holy statues including the statue of St Nepomuk by Richard Prachner goes

Church of the Knights of the Cross.

back to the plans of Jean Baptiste Mathey who brought a piece of French classicism to the Vltava. We are once again with the art of Bohemian Baroque painter Wenzel Lorenz Reiner in the church interior. The master has painted the depiction of the Last Judgement in the oval dome and in the spandrel, the four fathers of the church.

The Knights of the Cross lived according to the rules of St Augustine since 1252 at the Old Town bridge – head of Charles Bridge. They were in charge of the maintenance of the old Judith Bridge and collected customs and usage charges. This turned out to be a steady source of income for the prosperous and wealthy order that even the Hussite tumult could not harm.

The Knights of the Cross were well known for fostering church music. Willibald Gluck and Antonín Dvořák worked here as organists. A Knight of the Cross from the region of Znojmo, Karl Postl (1783–1864), became an important American author under the name Charles Sealsfield after fleeing the monastery.

Clementinum
[Klementinum, Křižovnická/ Karlova/Platnéřská, Praha 1]

The former Jesuit faculty spread over five courtyards and at least three churches belong to it: the **St Salvator Church**, the **St Clements Church** based on the plans of Kilian Ignaz Dientzenhofer

The Prague student
in the Clementinum.

library are set up in the Clementinum. Concerts are held in the splendid **Mirror Chapel**.

Emperor Ferdinand I summoned the Jesuits to Prague in 1556. The brothers of the order took over the Dominican monastery devastated during the Hussite wars in order to make progress with the Counter-Reformation from here. Although the Jesuits had been driven out of Prague several times they could finally assert themselves on the Vltava. In 1653 they laid the foundation for the Clementinum. Emperor Ferdinand III contributed a large part of the building costs for this ambitious project of enormous political importance then. Its dimension speaks for itself: after the Prague Castle the Clementinum is the largest building complex in the historic city.

where the first nativity scene in the country was exhibited in 1560 and the **Italian Chapel**, noteworthy due to its elliptical ground plan. The latter served the Italian congregation. The university and city

The Clementinum, as a Catholic university was meant to be the antipole to the Protestant oriented Charles University. After the victory of the Catholic troops at the White Mountain, the Jesuits also took over the Charles University.

The Clementinum.

But the triumph didn't last forever: the days of the Jesuits were also numbered under the rule of reformist Emperor Joseph II – the monks were forced to leave Prague. The Clementinum became an archi-episcopal seminary henceforth.

There is a monument commemorating the defence of Prague by students in 1648 made by the brothers Emanuel and Josef Calasanca Max in one of the Clementinum courtyards.

Church of St Salvator   71
[Kostel sv. Salvátora,
Karlova, Praha 1]

This church, belonging to the Clementinum complex, with its characteristic tri-section triumph arch was built in Renaissance style at the end of the 16th century. After Baroque additions in the 17th century the towers were built on in 1714.

The statues on the balustrade and on the gable (1659) are made by Johann Georg Bendl. Similarly the stucco adornments in the church interior and the sculptures of the twelve apostles at the confessionals are also by Bendl. The Jesuit historian Bohuslav Balbín who died in 1688 is buried in the church crypt.

Karlova Lane   72
[Karlova, Praha 1]

The connecting lane between the Charles Bridge and the Old Town Square, described as "Jesuits Lane" in its time, is now one of Prague's liveliest lanes. Despite the pushing and shoving between the shops many historically significant buildings ought not to be overlooked.

The lively Karlova Lane.

After the lost Battle of the White Mountain in 1621 the winter king Frederick of the Palatinate is believed to have taken flight from **Colloredo-Mansfeld Palace** [Karlova 2]. There is a beautiful Neptune fountain in the inner courtyard.

The astronomer Johannes Kepler lived and worked in the house **"At the French Crown"** [Karlova 4] between 1607 and 1612.

The wealthy publisher, printers and book dealer family Schönfeld had their seat in the **Schönfeld Palace** [Karlova 12].

House "At the Golden Well".

Prague's first coffee brewer Deodatus Damajan from Damascus had a flat in the Renaissance house **"At the Golden Snake"** [Karlova 18].

The first Prague cinema, the so-called "Biograph Ponrepo" [Karlova 20], was located in the rental Palace **"At the Blue Pike".**

The house **"At the Golden Well"** [Karlova 3] was formerly the papal nunciature. It has a magnificent Baroque façade with the portrayal of the medallion of the Virgin Mary of Stará Boleslav who is surrounded by the Bohemian SS Wenceslas, John of Nepomuk and the plague guardian SS Roch and Sebastian. The tympanum shows the plague guardian Rosalia lying in her grave.

St Salvator Church   73
[Kostel U Salvátora,
Salvátorská, Praha 2]

This hall church, built before the Thirty Years' War with the help of Protestant Christians throughout Europe, served the Lutherans

Shop adornment in the Karlova Lane.

from the Old Town. After the Battle of the White Mountain, it fell into the hands of the order of the Paulines; the Protestant preachers had to leave Prague. After the dissolution of the Pauline monastery in the Josephine period, the church was used as a mint for a short period. The St Salvator Church is the main church of the Bohemian Brethren Parish since 1918.

Church of the Holy Ghost `74`
[Kostel sv. Ducha,
Elišky Krásnohorské, Praha 1]

The Gothic church built in 1346 formerly belonged to one of the 1420 Benedictine monasteries destroyed by the Hussites. The church itself survived the Hussite wars but fell victim to a conflagration in 1689. On its reconstruction it was endowed with a Baroque vault. A simple statue of St Nepomuk by Ferdinand Maximilian Brokoff stands in front of the Church of the Holy Ghost.

Hospitallers Monastery `75`
[Klášter U Pavlánů,
U Milosrdných 1, Praha 1]

Towards the end of the Middle Ages there used to be a hospital on this spot. The Protestant Bohemian Brethren finally erected a hall church that was given to the Hospitallers after the Battle of the White Mountain. Accord-

ing to a local legend, the scaffolds for the execution of the 27 Bohemian gentlemen at the Old Town Square were made out of the planks and beams from a wooden stairwell in the hospital's interior. The Church of SS Simon and Juda belongs to the monastery. Wenzel Lorenz Reiner painted an altarpiece for this church. Because the Gothic church captivates with its excellent acoustics, it is now used for concerts. Joseph Haydn and Wolfgang Amadeus Mozart are supposed to have played on the church organ (ornamented with figures by Johann Brokoff).

St Agnes Convent `76`
[Anežský klášter,
U Milosrdných 17, Praha 1]

At the special wish of the devout Princess Agnes, daughter of the Bohemian King Přemysl Otakar I, the construction of a generous convent complex was begun in 1234 spreading over seven churches and two cloisters at the time. The Agnes Convent was allotted to the Franciscan order and divided into a monastery for the brothers of the Minorite order and the convent for the nuns of the order of St Clare. The founder Agnes herself with seven noble girls joined the latter and she was the abbess of the nuns of the order of St Clare from 1235 to 1237.
Princess Agnes, who was canonised several years ago and corresponded with St Clare, was known

St Salvator Church in
the St Agnes Convent.

Two of the churches in the complex are important burial churches: the grave of the convent founder Princess Agnes was found during restoration work in the St Salvator Church; King Wenceslas I is buried in the St Francis Church. The finding of the bones of Princess Agnes was of great symbolic importance, an old prophecy said: "When the body of the blessed Agnes is found in Prague, wars and unrests in Bohemia should stop and the country blossom in a golden era".

The National Gallery's collection of medieval arts in Bohemia and Central Europe that is worth seeing is exhibited in the St Agnes Convent.

for her humble and abstemious lifestyle even while she was alive. Not even Emperor Frederick II could convince her to trade her virginity for the imperial crown.

The convent was deserted during the Hussite unrest; however in the coming centuries, it developed into a regular monastery. In 1782 Emperor Joseph had this pious place shut down too. Towards the end of the 19th century, the disused buildings were so dilapidated that it was considered razing them to the ground.

After extensive restoration work lasting into the present times, the continued existence of this important architectural monument of Bohemian Gothic is guaranteed. A cloister, the chapter hall and the refectory from the times the convent was founded can still be viewed.

St Castulus Square and Church   77

[Haštalské náměstí a
kostel sv. Haštala, Praha 1]

An originally three-nave basilica from the 14th century dominates the peaceful square in the Old Town of Prague. The north nave was replaced by a remarkable two-nave hall, the structure is four-nave since. The church arches over dainty columns adorned with masks and plant decor. The tower rises from the south nave. A fire reduced this church to ash and debris in 1689, the reconstruction followed in a partly Baroque manner.

A Baroque calvary group by Ferdinand Maximilian Brokoff from 1716 belongs to the interior; Gothic wall panels have been maintained in the sacristy.

The Jewish Quarter
[Židovské město]

A Tour of the Jewish Quarter
[Pražské židovské město]

No one can say for certain when the Jews came to Bohemia, where and in what numbers they settled down. The beginnings lie in darkness. From written sources of the early Middle Ages it is evident that Jewish traders, physicians and civil servants lived in Prague. At least two Jewish settlements can be proved to have existed in the 10th and 11th centuries, one below the Prague Castle and another at Vyšehrad. After 1100 the Jewish community settled in the area of the Spanish Synagogue. The widely known Prague Jewish Town, the walled ghetto in the Old Town finally developed itself towards the end of the 12th century.

Prague Jewry experienced its heyday under the rule of Rudolph II when Mordechai Maisel, the mayor of the Jewish Town and the Emperor's court financier blessed with earthly goods, had the ghetto lanes paved, provided for deserted brides, had synagogues, schools, baths and the famous City Hall built and of course the Jewish Cemetery "Beth-Chajim" (House of Life) laid out. The esteemed Rabbi Loew worked and taught in the Prague Jewish Town around the same time – not only was he to go down in history as an important cabbalist and theologist but also as the creator of the Golem – at the centre of many legends. This creation of Rabbi

Loew, so the legend goes, stood on their side as an emergency helper in times of persecution.

On Easter 1389, the ghetto experienced one of the cruellest pogroms in the history of Prague Jewry. The walls of the Old-New Synagogue are supposed to have been coloured dark by the blood of those killed.

The entire Jewry was driven out of its inherited hometown twice: 1541 under the rule of Emperor Ferdinand I and 1744 under Maria Theresa's rule, who ordered by decree the expulsion of all Jews from Bohemia. Three years after the last families had left their

homes, the monarch found herself forced to revoke the expulsion decree. Only with the issue of the toleration edict by her son Joseph II did the situation change fundamentally for the Jews. The Jewish Town which is now called Josefov in his honour however fell into disrepair due to the moving away of affluent families to posher parts of the city. Evil dives, poverty and prostitution soon characterised the appearance of Josefov.

After several meetings and decisions a seminal cleanup was implemented about 1890, unfortunately a large part of the historical fabric was also ruined in the process. In place of the twisty dark lanes of the poor came the modern art nouveau palaces of rich citizens and industrialists. A generous boulevard, the Paris Street [Pařížská] was laid out – it is one of the poshest streets in the city even today.

The national socialist rulers eventually dealt the death blow to the Jewish community. Almost 80,000 Jews from the Reich Protectorate Bohemia-Moravia lost their lives in the occupation years between 1939 and 1945.

The Jewish Museum founded in 1906 manages a unique collection of diverse craft objects and documents. It is distributed in many buildings and synagogues. The Jewish Museum is closed for Sabbath – and so are all other institutions in the Jewish Town – on Saturdays.

Maisel Synagogue
[Maiselova synagoga,
Maiselova 10, Praha 1]

This synagogue also founded by Mordechai Maisel was considered the most magnificent building in the Jewish Town. The hall building supported on 20 columns was built by Josef Wahl and Juda Goldschmied in the Renaissance style around 1590. The temple was damaged in the great fire in the city in 1689 and was subsequently reconstructed in a Baroque manner. At the turn of the 20th century the synagogue was altered in the new Gothic style.

During the protectorate times, the temple served as the warehouse for confiscated furniture and articles from the houses and flats of displaced Jews. The synagogue now houses part of an exhibition about silver from Bohemian synagogues as well as the history of Bohemian and Moravian Jews.

Maisel Synagogue.

The Jewish City Hall **79**
[Židovská radnice,
Maiselova 18, Praha 1]

The Jewish City Hall built by
the Italian architect Pankraz Ro-
der in the 1680s is situated in
close proximity to the Old-New
Synagogue. The financial backer
for this building project was yet
again the rich primate Mordechai Maisel.

The City Hall houses the office
of the councillors of the Jewish
educational and cultural affairs,
and has a ritual dining hall as
well as the offices of the Prague
Jewish community. The Jewish
Museum with its unique collection of ritual textiles (curtains

from synagogues across Europe,
Torah coats etc.) is housed here.

After the Swedish siege in 1648
the Jews were granted the construction of the City Hall tower
as remarkable favour and reward
for active service in wartime. The
Town Hall was reconstructed in
1763 with a rococo façade and a
wooden tower. Two clocks adorned the tower, one with the Latin
and the other with Hebrew numbers that go from right to the left
like the Hebrew script.

The **City Hall Synagogue** bordering on the City Hall building
is also known as the "High Synagogue" [Vysoká synagoga] because the prayer room, a tasteful
late Renaissance hall, is situated
on the second floor.

Clock of the old Jewish City Hall.

The Old-New Synagogue 80

[Staronová synagoga,
Červená, Praha 1]

This temple is the oldest synagogue in Europe still serving its purpose. It was built by the royal stonemasons lodge in the 13th century. An entrance hall was added on at the beginning of the 14th century where the two counters for the tax officials were fitted in later. The tympanum decoration of the portal that symbolises the grapevine Israel with the roots of the twelve tribes is also from the 14th century.

The characteristic brick gable of the synagogue was added on to the existing building only in the 15th century. In the 18th century followed the addition of the side nave from where women could pursue the mass.

Going down the stairs one enters the synagogue interior that is divided into two naves by two octagonal pillars. The main hall was meant for men, a vestibule connected to the main prayer hall by small windows was intended for the women. Orthodox Jewish women were allowed to enter the synagogue on their wedding day only.

In the centre of the inner room is the Almemor, a rostrum from which the Torah is read and speeches to the community are delivered. An iron grille surrounds the altar room with a large nine-armed candelabrum. On the east wall is the Torah shrine surrounded by the Renaissance columns where the parchment scrolls with the five books of Moses are stored. Above it is another tympanum relief with vine leaves and tendrils.

The cross vault supported by columns is in five radials for a good reason: the Christian symbol of the cross was meant to be avoided in synagogical architecture.

Emperor Charles IV awarded the Prague community its own flag in 1358, the "High Banner". A flag from the 18th century exhibited in the synagogue commemorates this award.

5

Old-New Synagogue.

The Old Ceremonial Hall.

The Old Ceremonial Hall

81

[Obřadní síň,
U Starého hřbitova 3a, Praha 1]

Drawings made by children imprisoned in the ghetto Theresienstadt [Terezín] during the NS rule are exhibited in the new Romanesque building made of ashlar blocks at the entrance of the Old Jewish Cemetery in 1908. Most of these young artists were deported to the extermination camp in Auschwitz in autumn 1944. Only a few of the 15,000 girls and boys survived the prison camp.

The Old Jewish Cemetery "Beth Chaim"

82

[Starý židovský hřbitov,
Široká, Praha 1]

The Old Jewish Cemetery in Prague is the second oldest existing "Jewish Garden" in Europe apart from the Jewish cemetery in Worms. The oldest gravestone (1439) at the cemetery commemorates Avigdor Ben Isaak Kara, the chronicler of the Easter pogroms in 1389.

About 20,000 gravestones are layered on top of each other on these 11,000 m² grounds, the dead have been buried in about twelve layers on top of each other in the course of centuries. Pictorial depiction of the dead is forbidden in the Jewish faith, therefore carp, foxes, lions, bears, lancets, books, axes, cans etc. adorn the gravestones giving information of names, occupation or origin of the buried.

Visitors often leave little notes with various wishes written on them weighed down by little stones at the graves of known personalities. The grave of the rich primate of the Jewish Town Mordechai Maisel (died 1601) and the Renaissance tomb of the great Rabbi Je-

huda Loew Ben Bezalel (died 1609) are among the most interesting. Extraordinary too are the graves of the astronomer, physician and philosopher Josef del Medigo (died 1655), the scholar David Gans and Hendl Baschewi, wife of the magnate and first Bohemian Jew to be raised to nobility Jakob Baschewi "von Treuenburg".

The last burial took place in 1787. Burials within the city walls were forbidden in those days for hygienic reasons. The New Jewish Cemetery in Strašnice established in those days has been the last resting place of the Prague Jewry ever since.

At the Old Jewish Cemetery.

"Klausen" Synagogue [83]

[Klausová synagoga,
U Starého hřbitova, Praha 1]

Rabbi Jehuda Loew worked as the Talmud teacher in this plain synagogue financed by Mordechai Maisel on the grounds of the Old Jewish Cemetery. The synagogue originally consisted of three smaller buildings (Klausen) that were burned down in 1689. But its name was carried over to the successive building (built 1694 to 1696). The "Klausen" Synagogue was also a meeting place of the Prague Jewish undertakers. The Jewish Museum exhibits (about Jewish traditions and customs) are displayed here now.

Pinkas Synagogue

[Pinkasova synagoga, [84]
Široká, Praha 1]

The preceding building of the now Pinkas Synagogue was at that spot even in the 11th century; it could possibly be the oldest synagogue in Prague. The plot of land on which the synagogue was built in 1535, belonged to Rabbi Pinkas in the 14th century hence its name. About 1625, the Pinkas Synagogue was reconstructed in the manner of late Renaissance and was extended to include a conference hall and a women's gallery.

A monument for the victims of the NS rule was set up in the Pinkas Synagogue in the 1950s: the names of 77,297 murdered

Pinkas Synagogue.

Spanish Synagogue.

Jews from the Reich Protectorate Bohemia-Moravia were traced on the basis of the transportation files. The names were listed alphabetically according to place of origin and family on the walls of the main nave and the surrounding rooms.

Spanish Synagogue   85
[Španělská synagoga, Vězeňská 1, Praha 1]

In place of the synagogue burned down in 1389 replaced by a newly built "Altschul" (Old School) the perhaps oldest synagogue in Prague, a domed central structure in historic manner was constructed in 1882, the synagogue of the Jews living according to eastern rites. The gilded stuccowork interior, and the Moorish appearance of the temple made as a reproduction of the Spanish Alhambra, was intended to commemorate the Jews driven out of Spain who had found refuge in Prague for a while.

A monument for Franz Kafka was unveiled in close proximity

to the Spanish Synagogue in December 2003. The bronze statue by the Czech sculptor Jaroslav Rona shows the poet "riding" on the shoulders of a headless male figure.

Franz Kafka monument in Prague.

Arts and Crafts Museum **86**

[Uměleckoprůmyslové muzeum,
17. listopadu 2, Praha 1]

The largest glass collection in the world and significant furniture and craftwork made of metal, ceramics, textiles etc. exist in the building constructed for this purpose by architect Josef Schulz in 1901.

The museum is situated on the grounds of the historical Prague Jewish Town.

House of Artists **87**
Rudolfinum

[Dům umělců,
náměstí Jana Palacha 1, Praha 1]

The concert building made by the architects Josef Zítek and Josef Schulz in their representative neo-Renaissance style in 1880 acquired its name from the unlucky crown prince Rudolph of Habsburg. The members of the Czechoslovakian National Assembly debated in this magnificent building in the years 1918–1939, now the Rudolfinum serves the muses again under the name "House of Artists". Regular concerts including the Czech Philharmonic Orchestra are organised here and the famous music festival "Prague Spring" has found a home here. Sculptures of important composers like Wolfgang Amadeus Mozart and Felix Mendelssohn-Bartholdy are placed on the balustrade.

Adjacent to the Rudolfinum is a monument made by Bohumil Kafka in 1951 for the Czech painter Josef Mánes whose name the Mánes Bridge (1911) leading across to the Lesser Town also bears. A statue of the Czech composer Antonín Dvořák in front of the building looks at the obviously most splendid concert halls of the Czech Republic.

5

Concert Hall Rudolfinum.

The New Town
[Nové Město]

A Hike through the New Town
[Nové Město]

The New Town, established more than 650 years ago by Charles IV in 1348 in place of older settlements, can hardly do its name justice. Of course it is virginal as compared to the Old Town or the Prague Castle – the beginnings of which go back to the first century AD.

With the founding of the New Town, Emperor Charles IV gave the city Prague, bursting at the seams, further scope for development. He not only divided the course of the streets and squares but also dictated the location of the churches that were to be made of stone. The medieval regional development and traffic planning sufficed for the technical demands into the 20th century.

The New Town has in a way maintained a very youthful and lively atmosphere even today. Life in the capital is happening here, important business houses have their branches here and this is where the great political and cultural manifestations and revolutions took place especially in the 20th century.

Chic and elegance dominate the expensive and posh New Town with its central Wenceslas Square and nothing reminds one of the poor population that once eked out a wretched existence here and delivered a much fertilised

breeding ground for the Hussite movement. The Hussite turmoil was started in the Prague New Town. This part of town suffered damage from the unrest.

The middle-class residential area "Royal Vineyards" [Vinohrady] is also termed as the **"Upper New Town"**, an area where the wealth of the Gruenderzeit (1874–1914) is still evident.

Two churches ought to be viewed: the **Archdeaconry Church of St Ludmila** built by the cathedral master builder Josef Mocker 1888–1893 and also the **Church Most Sacred Heart of Our Lord** at the George of Poděbrady Square [náměstí Jiřího z Poděbrad] designed by the Slovene architect Josip Plečnik.

Wenceslas Square 88
[Václavské náměstí, Praha 1]

The square extends from Můstek at the border of the Old Town up to the Horse Gate that was situated where the National Museum is today. At the beginning of the 19th century the largest boulevard of Prague (750 x 60 m) was still surrounded by one to three-storey buildings, it took on the character of a capital city only in the 20th century. On the broad pavements of the shopping street flanked by limetree avenues, the young Prague meets tourists from all over the world. The judgement of the German poet Detlev von Liliencron, who termed Wenceslas Square the "World's proudest boulevard", is true even today. It was also known as "Horse Market" until 1848 because of the equestrian markets held here annually. The Czech journalist and author Karel Havlíček Borovský suggested renaming the boulevard to its present name Wenceslas Square in the revolution year 1848. That was intended to commemorate the revolutionary meetings in the so-called "Wenceslas Baths" that were situated there at the beginning of the June revolution in 1848. The Czechoslovakian Republic was proclaimed at the square, sloping upwards to the National Museum, on 28 October 1918. The masses gathered here in 1945, 1968 and 1989 partly in order to watch, partly to push ahead the respective political changes.

After the First World War there was a large vending machine, very modern for those times, in the art nouveau Palace **"Koruna"** [Václavské náměstí 1]. One could buy a meal for one crown here. The palace built in 1912 does not owe its name to the machine though, but to the splendid crown tower dominating the building. In the preceding building was the Café "Edison" that the American inventor visited during his stay in Prague.

Hotel Ambassador [Václavské náměstí 5] is an example of Prague art nouveau.

The **Baťa Building** [Václavské náměstí 6] is a constructivist building of the Moravian shoe factory owner Baťa from 1926. The passage enables thoroughfare to Jungmann Square.

"At the Golden Goose" [Zlatá husa, Václavské náměstí 7] is a posh Prague hotel enriched by tradition.

"Café Praha" [Václavské náměstí 10] is a constructivist coffeehouse built in 1929 that finds mention in Max Brod's social novels.

6

Koruna Palace at Wenceslas Square.

Franz Kafka began his career as an insurance employee in the Insurance Palace **"Assicurazioni Generali"** [Václavské náměstí 19].

Hotel Adria [Václavské náměstí 26] is a late Baroque building constructed in 1789.

The **Wiehl House** [Václavské náměstí 34] is a palace built in neo-Renaissance style by Antonín Wiehl in 1895/96. The wall adornments based on sketches of Mikoláš Aleš and Josef Fanta had to be renewed after their destruction in 1945.

Václav Havel and Alexandr Dubček held speeches during the "Velvet Revolution" (1989) from the Palace **"Melantrich"** [Václavské náměstí 36].

The **Lucerna Palace** [Václavské náměstí 38] was built by Václav Havel's grandfather during the First World War. This is the first reinforced concrete construction structure and has been the centre of Prague social life and a favourite venue for Balls since it was built.

Grandhotel Europa [Václavské náměstí 27] is an art nouveau hotel built in 1906 and has an elegant Café where Franz Kafka read from his narration *The Verdict*.

St Wenceslas Monument ▪89

[Pomník sv. Václava,
Václavské náměstí, Praha 1]

In 1912 a monumental statue of the Bohemian national patron St Wenceslas on horseback was placed at Wenceslas Square on the

St Wenceslas monument.

spot where a Baroque statue by Johann Georg Bendl (transferred to Vyšehrad in 1879) used to be. Surrounding the patron saint's horse are larger than life-size statues of SS Ludmila, Agnes, Procopius and Adalbert. The Czech sculptor Josef Václav Myslbek is believed to have worked on the monument for almost 30 years.

A series of memorable events of the national political history are closely connected with the statue of St Wenceslas on his steed. The Prague people in contrast are fond of "their horse" because the place "under the tail" is well-known as the venue for the gallant dates and lovers' rendezvous. Even "babička" (grandma) stood here in her young years with a throbbing heart … certainly not pondering over politics!

National Museum   **90**

[Národní muzeum,
Václavské náměstí 68, Praha 1]

National Museum.

The over 70 m high museum structure with the building front of 100 m was built in the neo-Renaissance shapes by Josef Schulz between 1885 and 1890. The mighty domed structure built in place of the former Horse Gate is of great symbolic importance for the Czech nation.

The main front with its statue-adorned ramp strikes the beholder; next to the enthroned Bohemia is the young girl embodying the Vltava and an old man personifying the Elbe. The fountain figures are flanked by allegories of Moravia and Silesia. Bohemia is once again portrayed in the tympanum as patron of arts and sciences. Allegorical statues (Willingness to Sacrifice, Enthusiasm, Love of Truth and the Past) by Bohuslav Schnirch are placed around the main dome.

The history section is on the first floor in the museum and the section for natural sciences on the second floor. The National Museum Library is the most important in the country with its stock

Wenceslas Square with the National Museum at night.

of almost one million volumes including valuable medieval manuscripts. The minerological-geological collections of the French geologist Joachim Barrande are of great value.

State Opera (formerly New German Theatre) 91
[Státní opera, Wilsonova 4, Praha 1]

Since 1859 there existed a wooden building on this site called "New Town Theatre" where performances were staged in the summer months. None other than Bedřich Smetana headed this makeshift theatre until 1882. The present neo-rococo opera house was built a few years later based on the plans of the very busy Viennese theatre architects Hermann Helmer and Ferdinand Fellner. The chariot of Dionysus and the muse Thalia are portrayed on the pediment of the classicist façade. Busts of Mozart, Goethe and Schiller stood beneath the pediment until the end of the Second World War.

The building erected on behalf of the German Theatre association under the influence of the Czech people's enthusiasm about the National Theatre was financed by private donations and collections. The inauguration was celebrated on 5th Jan. 1888 with Richard Wagner's *The Master-singers of Nuremberg* and within a short period of time this stage developed into a springboard for Austrian and Bohemian actors in the German-speaking region. The opera director Angelo Neumann from Bremen, appointed to the Vltava knew how to establish German Theatre of national importance in a mainly Czech city.

State Opera.

Central Station 92
[Hlavní nádraží, Wilsonova, Praha 1]

This central station, originally named after Emperor Francis Joseph, was built in 1901–1909 based on the plans of Josef Fanta. The four stone towers in the Prague Secession style lend it a distinctive appearance.

The green space lined with trees in front of the central station is the remnant of the former city park named after Jaroslav Vrchlický. The charm that must have been unique to it in about 1900 AD was lost through town planning

Prague Central Station.

measures in the 1970s. A plaque on the building Opletalova n° 41 initiated by the Austrian Society for Literature commemorates Franz Werfel who used to live in this area around the city park.

St Henry Church 93
[Kostel sv. Jindřicha,
Jindřišská, Praha 1]

Of the planned twin towers for the parish church in the Upper New Town, commissioned by Emperor Charles IV, only one tower was constructed. In a small garden, a former graveyard, isolated from the church stands the belfry with the bell "Maria" cast by the master Bartholomeus in 1518. The former defence tower was severely damaged during the Swedish siege.

On the three-nave church itself, that was regothicized with the church tower 1875–1879 by Jo-

sef Mocker, are sandstone figures of St John of Nepomuk and Judas Thaddeus by Michael Josef Brokoff. The altar panel in the church depicting the church patron Emperor Henry II with his wife St Kunigunde was created by Johann Georg Heintsch. Two paintings by Wenzel Lorenz Reiner are to be found in the Chapel of the Grievous Virgin Mary.

Old Customs Office "At the Hibernians" 94
[U Hybernů,
náměstí Republiky 3, Praha 1]

Irish Franciscan monks (Ireland Latin = Hibernia) who were expelled from their homeland under Queen Elizabeth's rule came to Prague in 1625 and found refuge in a Benedictine monastery that existed since 1359. Here they re-established the **St Ambrosius Church** that had been destroyed in the Hussite wars. By the time the former Baroque church acquired its splendid Empire façade (1808–1811), the Hibernian monastery was already secularised. The building has served as the tobacco depot, the main customs office and since the 1940s as an exhibition and trade fair hall.

The old customs office
"At the Hibernians".

"In the ditch" 95
[Na Příkopě, Praha 1]

The present shopping and promenade street between Powder Tower [Prašná brána] and Můstek at the lower end of Wenceslas Square gets its name from the ditch at this spot that until 1816 separated the Old Town from the New Town.

The **Czech National Bank** [Na Příkopě 28] was built in 1938 on the site of two hotels the "Blue Star" and the "Black Horse". Prominent guests like Hector Berlioz, Richard Wagner, Fyodor Dostoevsky and Carl Spitzweg stayed here. The Treaty of Prague was signed by Emperor William and Prince Bismarck at the hotel "The Blue Star" on 23rd August 1866.

The former "**German House at the Ditch**" was renamed "Slavic

"In the ditch".

House" [Slovanský dům] in 1945. The classicist remodelled Baroque palace had served the Prague Germans as a social centre since 1873. Several German organisations held their meetings here. Famous poets like Detlev von Liliencron, Rainer Maria Rilke and Gerhard Hauptmann read from their works in the Mirror Hall of the "German House".

On a visit to her native town Prague in 1895, the dedicated pacifist Bertha von Suttner held a recitation in the "German House" at the invitation of the organisation Concordia.

The **Palace of the Business Bank** [Na Příkopě 20] is richly decorated with statues and mosaics. Nostitz Palace where the Slavic Conference was held in 1848 once stood in its place.

Well-known personalities like Bernard Bolzano, Franz Werfel, Max Brod, Rainer Maria Rilke and Karel Hynek Mácha studied at the **Piarist Grammar School** [Na Příkopě 16].

The **Church of the Holy Cross** built 1816–1824 belonged to a former Piarist school and is considered a perfect example of empire style with the two Ionic columns in the façade.

There is a commemorative plaque at the **Czech Trade Bank** [Na Příkopě 14] for the Czech poetess Božena Němcová who died at the inn "At the Three Limetrees" (the preceding building) on 21st January 1862.

The Prague Literary Society (Egon Erwin Kisch, Max Brod, Ernst Weiß, Ludwig Winder, etc.) frequented the **"Café Continental"** [Na Příkopě 17] until the Second World War.

Palace Sylva-Taroucca [Na Příkopě 10] is a late Baroque palace with sculptural adornment by Ignaz Franz Platzer. The beautiful stairwell is also worth seeing.

Jungmann Square   96
[Jungmannovo náměstí, Praha 1]

This square is named after the founder of the modern Czech written language, Josef Jungmann (1773–1847) whose monument was put up here in 1878.

Church of St Mary   97
of the Snows
[Kostel Panny Marie Sněžné, Jungmannovo náměstí, Praha 1]

After his coronation as king of Bohemia, Charles IV established the Cathedral "St Mary of the Snows" in 1347. It was meant to be a landmark of the newly founded New Town and surpassed even the St Vitus Cathedral in its dimension. The choir was completed in 1397 but then the construction had to be stopped due to the Hussite wars. Since 1419 the radical preacher Jan Želivský worked in this church that had been taken over by the Hussites. In 1419 he led the demonstration procession to the New Town City Hall that was followed by the so-called "First Defenestration of Prague". The high church tower was destroyed in 1434 in the Hussite turmoil, the Gothic choir arch collapsed in the 16th century and had to be rebuilt as a result (1601).

The 35 m high choir towered over all the buildings in the New Town until the 19th century.

In the 20th century Prague's highest church disappeared forever amidst the towers and palaces of new business companies. The original impact can only be gauged from the Franciscan garden or from a higher vantage point.

In the interior of the "St Mary of the Snows", which has remained Gothic to a great extent, is a magnificent Baroque high altar with carvings and sculptures worth seeing. It is the largest of its kind in Prague. Wenzel Lorenz Reiner painted an altar panel (*The Annunciation*) for the northern side-altar.

The former **Franciscan monastery** [Jungmannovo náměstí 18] once housed the order of Carmelites, the Franciscans settled here about 1600. In the former monastery cellar is now a wine bar. The founders of the monastery King John of Luxembourg and his son Emperor Charles IV are portrayed on the cemetery portal towards the Wenceslas Square.

The inn **"At Pinkas"** [Jungmannovo náměstí 16] is in a middle-class Gothic building with a Renaissance portal. The Pilsner beer pub belonging to the former

tailormaster of the Franciscans, Jakub Pinkas, exists since 1843.

The author Anna Lauermann-Miksch (1852–1932) who published under the pseudonym Felix Téver, had a well-known literary salon – **"Salon Auermann"** – in a dainty Empire building [Jungmannovo náměstí 20].

National Street 98
[Národní třída, Praha 1]

The Insurance Palace **"Adria"** [Národní třída 40] was built in 1925 for the insurance company Riunione Adriatica. The world-famous "Laterna magica", a combination of theatre, music, pantomime, film and slide projection was originally housed here; it was first shown by its creator, the director Alfred Radok at the Brussels World Exhibition in 1958. The centre of the oppositional "Citizens Forum" met here during the "Velvet Revolution" in 1989.

During his visit to Prague, Bill Clinton played saxophone in the **"Jazzclub Reduta"** [Národní třída 20] – nameplates on the seats commemorate the session. **"Café Louvre"** where Franz Kafka was also a guest is on the first floor in the building.

The Cultural and Information Centre of the GDR had a seat in the **Insurance Palace Dunaj** [Národní třída 10], the constructivist palace from the twenties. The Prague author Gustav Meyrink lived in the preceding building, Wallis Palace.

Bedřich Smetana lived in **Lažanský Palace** [Národní třída 1] in 1868–1869. This is where his opera *The Bartered Bride* emerged. The artist and literature restaurant **"Café Slavia"** has been located in this building since 1881.

National Theatre **99**
[Národní divadlo,
Národní třída 2, Praha 1]

This theatre and opera house was inaugurated with Smetana's Opera *Libuše* on 11 June 1881 but a conflagration destroyed the building just two months after the ceremony. Nonetheless the nation was not to be discouraged: donations for the theatre were collected anew and on 14 April 1883 the tunes of the opera *Libuše* rang out once again for the gathered guests; this time the building was here to stay.

The National Theatre, with room for more than 1,800 spectators and built exclusively from local building material, belongs to the most magnificent neo-Renaissance constructions in Prague. Important artists of the time like the architect Josef Zítek, the painters Josef Mánes, Mikoláš Aleš, Hynais and Václav Brožík, the sculptors Bohuslav Schnirch and Josef Václav Myslbek contributed to the furnishings. They appear in Czech art history ever since as the "Generation of the National Theatre".

The aforementioned "Laterna magica" found a new home in the **Nová Scéna** (New Scene), a cube made of Cuban marble slabs behind glass annexed to the National Theatre built in the 1970s.

National Theatre on the Vltava.

St Adalbert Church [100]
[Farní chrám sv. Vojtěcha, Vojtěšská, Praha 1]

Not far from the National Theatre, close to the embankment, is the rarely noticed Gothic St Adalbert Church where ceiling panels from the first half of the 16th century have been found. The cross chapel originates from 1690. Antonín Dvořák played the church organ here between 1873 and 1876.

A memorial for the composer Josef Bohuslav Foerster (1859–1951) befriended with Gustav Mahler has been set up in the presbytery opposite which is adorned with the sculptures by Ignaz Franz Platzer.

New Town City Hall.

New Town City Hall [101]
[Novoměstská radnice, Karlovo náměstí, Praha 2]

The Gothic New Town City Hall is at the large Charles Square laid by Charles IV and formerly known as "Cattle Market". The First Defenestration of Prague on 30 July 1419 took place here. An infuriated crowd of followers of the reformer Jan Hus demanded the release of fellow believers on that day. As their demands were not met and they were moreover mocked, the enraged crowd stormed the official building and threw several Catholic councillors from a window of the City Hall. A total of 11 persons lost their lives in this incident. King Wenceslas was filled with indignation at that and died of the stroke a few days later.

Church of SS Cyril and Methodius [102]
[Kostel sv. Cyrila a Metoděje, Resslova, Praha 2]

The church – formerly St Charles Borromeus Church – probably owes its Baroque flourish to Kilian Ignaz Dientzenhofer. The Czech parachutists responsible for the assassination attempt on the deputy Reich Protector Reinhard Heydrich (27 May 1942) met their death here on 18 June 1942. The pursuers' attention was drawn to the church where the assassins were hiding in the crypt by a hint from a traitor.

A small museum and a memorial plaque fitted in the wall commemorate the events.

and the roof terrace restaurant are open to the public.

Emaus Monastery [104]
[Emauzský klášter,
Vyšehradská 49, Praha 2]

Even this Benedictine monastery founded by Charles IV as a safe keeping place for the Slavic liturgy ("At the Slaves"– Na Slovanech) fell into disrepair during the Hussite times. This monastery was consecrated on Easter Monday 1372 and therefore its name reminds of the Easter gospel in which the journey of the disciples to Emaus is mentioned. The Baroque towers of the monastery church were destroyed in an American bomb raid in February 1945. The cycle of frescoes in the monastery cloister created by the court painters of Charles IV were severely damaged in the firefighting operations.

The Dancing House.

Dancing House [103]
[Tančící dům,
Rašínovo nábřeží 80, Praha 2]

The futuristic building by the American architect Frank O. Gehry was built in the mid-90s on a plot that stood unused for decades, a gaping hole left by bombs in the Second World War. The two cylindrical structures of the building, jokingly called Ginger Rogers and Fred Astaire, contrast somewhat importunately with the surrounding almost uniform turn-of-the-century architecture. The experts categorise the building as "deconstructivist disastrous architecture". The Dancing House is presently used as office premises, only the ground floor

Charles Church [105]
[Karlov, Ke Karlovu 1, Praha 2]

Emperor Charles IV had the high Gothic structure erected in 1350 to commemorate his coronation in Aachen and ascribed it to the canons of the Augustine order summoned from France. After over two decades of construction, the church was consecrated in 1377 to Charles the Great and the Assumption. The Hussites destroyed the church in 1420; after more than 70 years though the church could be consecrated anew and serve its purpose. Charles Church developed into a Baroque pilgrimage place in the 17th century.

The Outskirts
[Na předměstí]

On the Outskirts

Vyšehrad
[Vyšehrad, Praha 2]

106

The citadel Vyšehrad, a Baroque fortification lies calm and mysterious on a rocky ledge high above the Vltava embankment. It is presumed that here, to the south of Prague there already existed an old Slavic castle in the eighth century; the first written mention though is in the chronicles from the year 1002. In the course of the century long history, Vyšehrad was the royal seat, a small market town, Bohemia's religious centre (Vyšehrad's provost was, apart from the archbishop, the second highest personality in the ecclesiastical order of precedence),

Baroque fortress and outing destination for the capital's residents. A row of buildings and monuments remind one of the eventful history of the hill.

St Martin Rotunda.

The **St Martin Rotunda** from the 11th century is the oldest Prague Rotunda still in good condition.

The wall and rock remnants jetting out over the River Vltava are known as **"Libuše's Bath"**. The prophetess Libuše is believed to have gone down from here to bathe in the river.

Leopold Gate reminds one of the time when Vyšehrad was a mighty military stronghold complex.

The **Old Deanery** [Soběslavova 1] was the residence of this chapter's Dean. It was severely

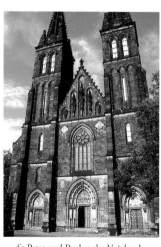

St Peter und Paul at the Vyšehrad.

damaged in a gunpowder explosion in 1760.

The **New Deanery** [Štulcova 4] and was built in a neo-Gothic manner in the years 1872–1874 by Provost Václav Štulc.

The **Chapter- and Parish Church of St Peter and Paul** has a construction history reaching back to the Middle Ages. The façade was renewed in the 20th century and a neo-Gothic portal (with the relief of the Last Judgement) was added. Inside the church is a copy of the Rain Madonna.

The **Slavín** is a monument of the Vyšehrad cemetery. Important personalities of Czech cultural life like Jan Neruda, Alfons Mucha, Bedřich Smetana, Antonín Dvořák, Karel Hynek Mácha, Mikoláš Aleš etc. lie buried here.

Villa Bertramka 107
[Bertramka, Mozartova 2, Praha 5]

Villa Bertramka is a small former vineyard in Smíchov, a suburb outside the city walls. Mozart was a guest of his Prague friends František and Josepha Dušek in the idyllic country house in 1787. His opera *Don Giovanni,* that held its premier performance in the Estates Theatre, is believed to have been completed in the Villa Bertramka.

The villa is a museum now and without doubt the most important Mozart memorial in Prague. Mozart's stays in Prague can be followed in stages in seven exhibition rooms: amongst others, there is a grand piano Mozart was supposed to have played on. There is a statue commemorating the composer in the garden on the estate.

7

Mozart-Villa „Bertramka".

Hanau Pavilion on the Letná Hill.

"Belvedere"- Heights 108
[Letná, Praha 6]

As the name itself indicates: this plateau over the River Vltava offers a beautiful view and is a charming outing destination especially in summer. Several little sights strike us while strolling in the park complex: the **residence of the head of the government** (Kramář Villa), the peculiar **Hanau Pavilion** (cast in Prince Wilhelm of Hanau's ironworks on the occasion of the Jubilee National Exhibition 1891), the inordinately large **metronome** on a concrete plinth that adorns the largest Stalinist monument ever in the 1950s; the monumental statue was blown up without more ado as soon as the days of the tyrant were gone by.

The communist government presented itself on 1ˢᵗ May every year with parades and march past on the large **Letná plateau**. Hundreds of thousands of Czechs protested against the regime here in 1989.

Žižka Monument 109
[Národní památník Jana Žižky na Vítkově, Praha 3]

A mighty figure on horseback in front of the granite covered cube is visible from afar on Vítkov Hill also known as Žižkov Hill. The national monument erected between 1927 and 1932 consists, besides the main hall and the President's Grave, also the Grave of the Unknown Soldier. The 9 m high statue of a man mounted on a horse placed there in 1950 is a monument for the Hussite Commander Jan Žižka of Trocnov who triumphed over the Catholic Emperor Sigismund in 1420. The statue based on a model created by Bohumil Kafka is the largest equestrian statue cast in bronze in the world.

Troja Chateau 110
[Zámek Troja,
U Trojského zámku 1, Praha 8]

The Summer Residence Troja, one of the magnificent palaces in the country and at the same time a masterpiece of Bohemian Baroque, was built in the years 1680–1688 for Count Wenzel Adalbert of Sternberg. The architect Jean Baptiste Mathey had a three-winged complex erected based on the French example, at the same time implementing the impressions of the years he had spent in Rome. The Troja Chateau has a uniquely beautiful open stairway with figures from Greek mythology, taking as a theme the triumph of the Olympic gods over the Gigants (Gigantomachie). The splendidly painted **banquet**

7

Chateau Troja.

171

hall (Imperial Hall) with the gallery of ancestral portraits of the reigning family Habsburg, scenes from Austrian history (for example, Victory of Austrians over Turks) as well as heraldic and allegorical portrayals, is the centre and the climax of the late Baroque chateau complex.

> The Gallery of the Capital Prague also exhibits Czech art of the 19th century in the chateau.

> Troja Chateau was built in place of old vineyards; wine is grown in the surrounding area even today. Nature lovers can not only visit the Pomological Institute (Institute for fruit-growing) but also the Prague Zoo as well as the Orchard [Stromovka], one of the most attractive garden complexes in Central Europe.

Portal to Břevnov Monastery.

Břevnov Monastery   111

[Klášter sv. Markéty v Břevnově, Bělohorská, Praha 6]

The Benedictine abbey is the oldest monastery in Prague and at the same time the starting point for many subsidiaries in the country. The abbey was founded by the second Bishop of Prague, Bishop Adalbert in 992 AD. The first monks came from Italy; they brought relics of SS Alexius and Bonifacius with them. The relics of St Margaret, to whom the monastery church is dedicated, were also brought to Břevnov later on. The present **monastery church** was erected at the beginning of the 18th century by Christoph Dientzenhofer. Only the crypt remained of the preceding early Romanesque building. The altar pieces in the monastery church are from Peter Brandl. They deal with the themes *Death of St Benedict* as well as *Death of the Blessed Günther*, one of the hermits buried here. A ceiling fresco in the **prelate hall** of the monastery is also dedicated to the death of this devout hermit. The master of south German late Baroque Cosmas Damian Asam painted the fresco.

Summer Residence Hvězda   112

[Letohrádek Hvězda, obora Hvězda, Praha 6]

Emperor Ferdinand I had a game enclosure laid out and surrounded with a protective wall on the outskirts of the city in 1530. His son Archduke Ferdinand of Tyrol then had the Summer Residence Hvězda (Czech word for star) built in the Renaissance style in 1555. He chose to give it the shape of a six-radial star.

The ground floor has stucco work by Paolo della Stella. The second floor consisted of living rooms; the third floor is a 12-sided fresco adorned and cupola vaulted hall with a relief decorated ceiling. The historical Battle of the White Mountain, where the Protestant Bohemian estates were defeated by the Catholic league, was fought on grounds nearby.

A museum for the author Alois Jirásek (1851–1930) and the painter Mikoláš Aleš (1852–1913) is housed in the Summer Residence Hvězda.

Church of Maria Victoria at the White Mountain
[Kostel Panny Marie Vítězné na Bílé hoře, Karlovarská 3/6, Praha 6]

This pilgrimage church is situated at the spot where the Bohemian estates army suffered a decisive defeat against the imperial troops led by Maximilian of Bavaria on 8 November 1620. Two years after the battle, a chapel was erected here.

The St Mary Shrine is in the middle of the cloister full of portraits and paintings depicting the miracles of the Holy Virgin. An old Carmelite father allegedly carried the painting *Mary of Victory* in the victorious battle. The church frescoes originate among others from Wenzel Lorenz Reiner.

A small stone pyramid not far from the church commemorates the exact place of the battle.

Summer Residence Hvězda.

Recommended Day Trips

Karlštejn Castle.

By train: With metro line B to Smíchov Station [Smíchovské nádraží], and by train to Karlštejn from there.

Theresienstadt [Terezín]

This concentration camp situated 45 km northwest of Prague was a garrison town until the Second World War. More than 150,000 people were brought here during the Second World War, lost their lives in the ghetto town or the "Little Fortress" or were deported to the extermination camp Auschwitz.

Info: Městské informační centrum, náměstí Čs. armády 179. Tel.: 416 782 616
Getting there: By car or by bus via motorway D 8.

Karlštejn

The main road of the village leads up to the castle where Charles IV had the coronation jewels in safekeeping. Today, this castle is the main tourist attraction outside Prague. The panel paintings by Master Theodoric are worth seeing.
The castle is open daily except Mondays.
Closed in January and February
Information: 311 681 695
Getting there by car: 38 km via motorway D 5.

Kutná Hora

The Silver City was of great significance in the Middle Ages. The *Prague Groschen* was made in the mint here. This little country town is an attraction for travellers because of its intact Old Town and

In the "small fortress" in Theresienstadt [Terezín].

St Barbara Cathedral in Kutná Hora.

A look at the wine-town Mělník.

the magnificent St Barbara Cathedral. The short trip is worthwhile for a view of the architectonic treasures and a walk-in mine.
Info: Městské kulturní a informační centrum [City Culture and Information Centre].
Tel.: 327 512 378
Getting there: 68 km east of Prague (via road 333)

Zbraslav

Many foreigners come to this Cistercian monastery founded in 1291 because of a collection of sculptures and an exhibition of Asian art. A visit is recommended especially in summer.
Info: Městský úřad
Tel.: 546 453 198
Getting there: 10 km outside Prague (via road 4)

Mělník

The wine town situated at the confluence of the Elbe River and the Vltava was the personal estate of the Bohemian queens. The castle owned by the Lobkowicz family is known for its good restaurant, wines from the surrounding areas are served from their own wine cellar. The "Ludmila" wines are especially popular for their characteristic bottles.
Tel.: 315 626 650
Getting there: 38 km to the north (via road 9)

Konopiště

The castle was once owned by the Austrian crown prince Francis Ferdinand d'Este who could indulge in his passion – unrestrained hunting. Secret negotiations took place here between Francis Ferdinand, Emperor William II and Admiral Alfred von Tirpitz.
Tel.: 317 721 198
Getting there: 44 km towards Benešov (via motorway E 14)

Křivoklát

The beautiful castle complex from the 11th century is situated in the middle of a forested hiking region.
Tel.: 313 558 440
Getting there: 46 km towards Beroun (via motorway E 12)

Lidice

This village was razed to the ground on 10th June 1942 as revenge for the assassination of the deputy Reich Protector Reinhard Heydrich. The men were killed by a shooting commando, the women taken to the concentration camp Ravensbrück, the children were mostly sent to the Reich to be "Germanised". Lidice was rebuilt after the Second World War in close proximity of the old, completely destroyed village. A memorial was erected in place of the historical Lidice.
Info: Obecní úřad
Tel.: 312 253 083
Getting there: 22 km towards Kladno (via road 7)

8

Brief Czech Guide

In general

yes	ano
no	ne
please	prosím
thank you	děkuji
excuse me	promiňte
large	velký
small	malý
young	mladý
new	nový
old	starý

Numbers

0	nula
1	jeden, jedna, jedno
2	dva, dvě
3	tři
4	čtyři
5	pět
6	šest
7	sedm
8	osm
9	devět
10	deset
11	jedenáct
12	dvanáct
13	třináct
14	čtrnáct
15	patnáct
16	šestnáct
17	sedmnáct
18	osmnáct
19	devatenáct
20	dvacet
30	třicet
40	čtyřicet
50	padesát
60	šedesát
70	sedmdesát
80	osmdesát
90	devadesát
100	sto
200	dvěstě
1000	tisíc
2000	dva tisíce

Days of the Week

Monday	pondělí
Tuesday	úterý
Wednesday	středa
Thursday	čtvrtek
Friday	pátek
Saturday	sobota
Sunday	neděle

Months

January	leden
February	únor
March	březen
April	duben
May	květen
June	červen
July	červenec
August	srpen
September	září
October	říjen
November	listopad
December	prosinec

Seasons

spring	jaro
summer	léto
autumn	podzim
winter	zima

Getting acquainted

Good morning!	Dobré ráno!
Good day!	Dobrý den!
Good evening!	Dobrý večer!
Good night!	Dobrou noc!
Goodbye!	Na shledanou!
Bye!	Ahoj!
What's your name?	Jak se jmenujete?
My name is ...	Jmenuji se ...
How old are you?	Kolik je Vám let?
I'm ... years old.	Je mi ... let.
Where are you from?	Odkud jste?
I'm from the UK.	Jsem z Velké Británie.
Do you speak English?	Mluvíte anglicky?
How are you?	Jak se máte?
I'm fine.	Mám se dobře.
I speak very little Czech.	Mluvím česky jen trochu.
I don't understand.	Nerozumím.
Once again, please.	Ještě jednou, prosím.

Directions

north	sever

south	jih
east	východ
west	západ
left	nalevo
right	napravo
up	nahoře
down	dole
straight on	rovně
back	zpátky
far	daleko
nearby	blízko
How far is ...?	Jak daleko je ...?
How can I get to ...?	Jak se dostanu ...?
Where is ...?	Kde je ...?

Travelling by train

train station	nádraží
platform	kolej
train	vlak
ticket	jízdenka
When does the train to Brno leave?	Kdy jede vlak do Brna?
Is this seat still free?	Je to místo volné?
Where is the central station?	Kde je hlavní nádraží?
Is this the price for a return ticket?	Platí tato cena za cestu tam i zpět?

Driving by car

departure	odjezd
breakdown service	odtahová služba
car	auto
motorway	dálnice
unleaded	natural (bez olova)
diesel	nafta
breakdown	porucha
car park	parkoviště
street	ulice
super	super
fill up	tankovat
petrol station	benzinová pumpa
leaded	olovnatý
garage	autoopravna
How can I get to the motorway to ...?	Jak se dostanu na dálnici na ...?

Food and drink

apple	jablko
apple juice	jablečná šťáva
banana	banán
beef	hovězí maso
beer	pivo
bottle	láhev
bread	chléb
breakfast	snídaně
broccoli	brokolice
butter	máslo
cauliflower	květák
cheese	sýr
cherries	třešně
chicken	kuře
coffee	káva
coffee with milk	káva s mlékem
cucumber	okurek
dessert	moučník
duck	kachna
dumplings	knedlíky
egg	vejce
fish	ryba
fried sausage	klobása
fruit juice	džus
glass	sklenice
goose	husa
grapes	hroznové víno
ham	šunka
icecream	zmrzlina
jam	marmeláda
lemon	citron
lobster	humr
meat	maso
milk	mléko
mineralwater	minerálka
mushrooms	houby
oil	olej
orange juice	pomerančový džus
pear	hruška
pepper	pepř
plums	švestky
pork	vepřové maso
potatoes	brambory
poultry	drůbež
red cabbage	červené zelí
red wine	červené víno
rice	rýže
roast	pečeně
roast pork	vepřová pečeně
roast veal	telecí pečeně
roll	rohlík
rosé wine	rosé
salad	salát
salmon	losos
salt	sůl
sauerkraut	kyselé zelí
sausage	salám
seafood	mořský salát
small sausages	párky
smoked meat	uzené maso
soup	polévka
starters	předkrm

strawberry	jahoda
sugar	cukr
sweets	sladkosti
tea	čaj
trout	pstruh
tuna	tuňák
turkey	krůta
veal	telecí maso
vegetables	zelenina
vinegar	ocet
watermelon	meloun
whipped cream	šlehačka
white cabbage	hlávkové zelí
white wine	bílé víno
wine	víno

In a Restaurant

menu	jídelní lístek
dry wine	suché víno
sweet wine	sladké víno
dark beer	černé pivo
lager	světlé pivo
knife	nůž
fork	vidlička
spoon	lžíce
napkin	ubrousek
Where can I find	Kde najdu
a good restaurant	dobrou restauraci
(with Czech cuisine)?	(s českou kuchyní)?

The menu, please.	Jídelní lístek, prosím.
What can you recommend?	Můžete mi něco doporučit?
Do you have something vegetarian?	Máte nějaká vegetariánská jídla?
May one smoke here?	Může se zde kouřit?
I would like ...	Dám si ...
The bill, please.	Účet, prosím.

Overnight stay

hotel	hotel
youth hostel	ubytovna (hostel)
double-room	dvoulůžkový pokoj
single-room	jednolůžkový pokoj
shower	sprcha
toilet	záchod
half board	polopenze
full board	plná penze
reservations	rezervace
I have booked a room.	Rezervoval jsem pokoj.
Do you still have	Máte ještě

a vacant room?	volné pokoje?
Do you have a room for one night?	Máte pokoj na jednu noc?
Are pets allowed?	Je možné vzít s sebou domácí zvířata?

In the city

bank	banka
bridge	most
castle	hrad
shopping street	nákupní ulice
garden	zahrada
shop	obchod
island	ostrov
church	kostel
museum	muzeum
opera	opera
park	park
square	náměstí
post office	pošta
palace	zámek
call-box	telefonní budka
theatre	divadlo
change Bureau	směnárna

Pronunciation

á, **é**, **í**, **ó**, **ú**, **ů**, **ý**	are long vowels
c	is pronounced **ts** as in boots
č	pronounced **ch** as in child
ck	pronounced **tsk** as in německy – *nye-metske*
ě	used after a consonant, pronounced **ye** as in yes.
ř	especially difficult sound, pronounced as a combination of **r** and **sh** (as in Dvořák – *Dvor-shak*)
r	rolled sound
š	**sh** as in shack
ž	as in vision

Service Section

Embassies and Consulates

Austria
Viktora Huga 500/10
151 15 Praha 5
Tel.: 257 090 511 / Fax: 257 316 045
www.austria.cz

Belgium
Valdštejnská 152/6
118 01 Praha 1
Tel.: 257 533 524 / Fax: 257 533 750
Ambabel-Prague@mbox.vol.cz

Brazil
Sušická 1850/12
160 41 Praha 6
Tel.: 224 324 965 / Fax: 224 312 901
chebrem@mbox.vol.cz

Canada
Muchova 6
160 00 Praha 6
Tel.: 272 101 800 / Fax: 272 101 890
AmbCanada2@quick.cz
www.canada.cz

Cyprus
Sibiřské náměstí 754/6
160 00 Praha 6
Tel.: 224 316 833 / Fax: 224 317 529
cyprusembass@mbox.vol.cz

Denmark
Maltézské náměstí 475/5
118 01 Praha 1
Tel.: 257 531 600 / Fax: 257 531 410
www.ambprag.un.dk

Estonia
Na Kampě 1
118 00 Praha 1
Tel.: 257 011 180 / Fax: 257 011 181
embassy.prague@estemb.cz

Finland
Hellichova 458/1
118 00 Praha 1
Tel.: 251 177 251 / Fax: 251 177 241
www.finland.cz

France
Velkopřevorské náměstí 486/2
118 01 Praha 1
Tel.: 251 171 711 / Fax: 251 171 720
www.france.cz

Germany
Vlašská 347/19
118 01 Praha 1
Tel.: 257 531 481 / Fax: 257 534 056
www.german-embassy.cz

Great Britain
Thunovská 180/14
118 00 Praha 1
Tel.: 257 402 111 / Fax: 257 402 296
info@britain.cz
www.britain.cz

Greece
Helénská 1781/2
120 00 Praha 2
Tel.: 222 250 955 / Fax: 222 253 686
greekemb@czn.cz

Hungary
Českomalínská 7/20
160 00 Praha 6
Tel.: 233 324 454 / Fax: 233 322 104
huembprg@vol.cz

Ireland
Tržiště 366/13
118 00 Praha 1
Tel.: 257 530 061-4 / Fax: 257 531 387
irishembasy@iol.cz

Israel
Badeniho 2
170 01 Praha 7
Tel.: 233 097 500 / Fax: 233 097 519
www.prague.mfa.qov.il

Italy
Nerudova 214/20
118 00 Praha 1
Tel.: 233 080 111 / Fax: 257 531 522
www.italianembassy.cz

Japan
Maltézské náměstí 6
118 01 Praha 1
Tel.: 257 533 546 / Fax: 257 532 377
www.cz.emb-japan.go.jp

Latvia
Hradešínská 3
101 00 Praha 10
Tel.: 255 700 881 / Fax: 255 700 880
www.prague.am.qov.lv

Lithuania
Pod Klikovkou 1916/2
150 00 Praha 5
Tel.: 257 210 122 / Fax: 257 210 124
ambasada-litva@iol.cz

Luxembourg
Tržiště 13
118 00 Praha 1
Tel.: 257 181 800 / Fax: 257 532 537
www.ambalux.cz

Malta (Consulate)
Perlová 1
110 00 Praha 1
Tel.: 221 667 360 / Fax: 221 667 387

Netherlands
Gotthardská 27/6
160 00 Praha 6
Tel.: 233 015 200 / Fax: 233 015 254
www.netherlandembassy.cz

Norway
Hellichova 458/1
118 00 Praha 1
Tel.: 257 323 737 / Fax: 257 326 827
www.noramb.cz

Poland
Valdštejnská 153/8
118 01 Praha 1
Tel.: 257 530 388 / Fax: 257 530 135
ambrprczechy@mbox.vol.cz

Portugal
náměstí Kinských 76/7
150 00 Praha 5
Tel.: 257 311 230-1 / Fax: 257 311 234
www.embportugal.cz

Russia
Pod Kaštany 19/1
160 00 Praha 6
Tel.: 233 374 100 / Fax: 233 377 235
www.czech.mib.ru

Slovakia
Pod Hradbami 666/1
160 00 Praha 6
Tel.: 233 113 051 / Fax: 233 113 054
www.slovakemb.cz

Slovenia
Pod Hradbami 659/15
160 41 Praha 6
Tel.: 233 081 211 / Fax: 224 314 106
vpr@mzz-dkp.gov.si

Spain
Badeniho 401/4
170 00 Praha 7
Tel.: 224 311 441 / Fax: 233 341 770
EmbPraha@gts.cz,
Praga@Embajadas.mae.es

Sweden
Úvoz 156/13
118 01 Praha 1
Tel.: 220 313 200 / Fax: 220 313 240
www.swedenabroad.com/praha

Switzerland
Pevnostní 588/7
162 00 Praha 6
Tel.: 220 400 611 / Fax: 224 311 312
Vertretung@pra.rep.admin.ch

Ukraine
Charlese de Gaulla 916/29
160 00 Praha 6
Tel.: 233 342 000 / Fax: 233 344 366
www.uaembassy.cz

USA
Tržiště 15
118 01 Praha 1
Tel.: 257 530 663 / Fax: 257 530 583
www.usembassy.cz

Accommodation and Tourist Information

A website in several languages giving interesting information about trips to Prague: www.visitprague.cz (last-minute-hotel reservations, accommodation, special offers, tours, general information etc.).

Pražská informační služba (PIS)
Betlémské náměstí 2
116 98 Praha 1
Tel.: 124 44
tourinfo@pis.cz
www.pis.cz

Pražská informační služba (PIS)
Na Příkopě 20
110 00 Praha 1
Tel.: 221 714 444
Fax: 224 230 783
info@avetravel.cz
www.avetravel.cz

Pragotur
Arbesovo náměstí 4
150 00 Praha 5
Tel.: 221 714 130
Fax: 221 714 127
pragotur@pis.cz
www.pis.cz

AVE
Wilsonova 8
120 00 Praha 2
Tel.: 224 223 226
Fax: 224 230 783
centrala@avetravel.cz
www.phl.cz

Accommodation and tourist information at the **Main Central Station**.
Daily from 6 a.m.–11 p.m.
www.avetravel.cz

Hotels (expensive category)

Category *****

Four Seasons
Veleslavínova 2a
110 00 Praha 1
Tel.: 221 427 000 / Fax: 221 426 666
prg.reservations@fourseasons.com
www.fourseasons.com/prague/index.html

Marriott
V Celnici 8
111 21 Praha 1
Tel.: 222 888 888 / Fax: 222 888 889
prague.reservations@marriotthotels.com
www.marriott.com/PRGDT

Renaissance
V Celnici 7
111 21 Praha 1
Tel.: 221 822 100 / Fax: 221 822 200
renaissance.prague@renaissancehotels.com
www.gestin.cz or
www.renaissancehotels.com

Carlo Boscolo IV. Luxury
Senovážné náměstí 13
110 00 Praha 1
Tel.: 224 593 111 / Fax: 224 593 000
reservations@carloIV.boscolo.com
www.boscolohotels.com

InterContinental
náměstí Curieových 5
110 00 Praha 1
Tel.: 296 631 111 / Fax: 224 810 071
pratur@interconti.com
www.interconti.com

Hilton
Pobřežní 1
186 00 Praha 8
Tel.: 224 841 111 / Fax: 224 842 378
mail@hilton-prague.czwww.hilton.com

Paříž
U Obecního domu 1
110 00 Praha 1
Tel.: 222 195 195 / Fax: 222 195 906
pariz@hotel-paris.cz
www.hotel-pariz.cz

Radisson SAS Alcron
Štěpánská 40
110 00 Praha 1
Tel.: 222 820 000 / Fax: 222 820 100
Sales.prague@radissonsas.com
www.radissonsas.com

Grand Hotel Bohemia
Králodvorská 4
110 00 Praha 1
Tel.: 224 804 111 / Fax: 222 329 545
office@grandhotelbohemia.cz
www.grandhotelbohemia.cz

Category ****

Adria
Václavské náměstí 26
110 00 Praha 1
Tel.: 221 081 111 / Fax: 221 081 300
accom@adria.cz
www.hoteladria.cz

Ambassador
Zlatá husa
Václavské náměstí 5–7
111 24 Praha 1
Tel.: 224 193 111 / Fax: 224 226 167
hotel@ambassador.cz
www.ambassador.cz

Diplomat
Evropská 15
160 41 Praha 6
Tel.: 296 559 111 / Fax: 296 559 215
hotel@diplomatpraha.cz
www.diplomat-hotel.cz

Don Giovanni
Vinohradská 157a
130 20 Praha 2
Tel.: 267 031 111 / Fax: 267 036 717
Info.PRGDON@dorint.com
www.dorint.com

Crowne Plaza
Koulova 15
160 45 Praha 6
Tel.: 296 537 111 / Fax: 296 537 847
hotel@crowneplaza.cz
www.crowneplaza.cz

U Páva
U Lužického semináře 32
118 00 Praha 1
Tel.: 257 533 360 / Fax: 257 530 919
upava@romantichotels.cz

U Tří pštrosů
Dražického náměstí 12
118 00 Praha 1
Tel.: 257 532 410 / Fax: 257 533 217
info@upstrosu.cz
www.upstrosu.cz

Villa Voyta
K Novému dvoru 54
142 00 Praha 4
Tel.: 261 711 307-8 / Fax: 244 471 248
info@villavoyta.cz
www.villavoyta.cz

U Krále Karla
Nerudova-Úvoz 4
118 00 Praha 1
Tel.: 257 533 594 / Fax: 257 531 049
ukralekarla@romantichotels.cz
www.romantichotels.cz/ukralekarla/

Hostels and Pensions

The website www.hostelprague.com (English) offers an overview of Prague hostels and cheap youth hostels. Another website for travellers seeking accommodation is www.accommodationinczech.com. Reservations can also be made through this address.

Ritchie's Hostel
Karlova 9–13
110 00 Praha 1
Tel.: 222 221 229
Fax: 222 220 255
ritchie@centrum.cz
www.ritchieshostel.cz
This hostel is located in Prague centre between Charles Bridge and Old Town Square. The rooms are simple but clean.

Junior Hostel
Senovážné náměstí 21
110 00 Praha 1
Tel.: 233 353 742
junior@prague-hostels.cz
www.junior.prague-hostels.cz
This hostel is located in the city centre close to Wenceslas Square.

Hostel Vesta
Wilsonovo nádraží
110 00 Praha 1
vesta@prague-hostels.cz
www.vesta.prague-hostels.cz
This accommodation is located in the historical building of the Central Station.

Pension Beetle
Šmilovského 10
120 00 Praha 2
Tel.: 222 515 093
Fax: 222 515 093
beetle@beetle-tour.cz
www.beetle-tour.cz/beetle
Located in the picturesque Vinohrady area, one can reach the Prague city centre in about 15 minutes.

Hotel U Sladků
Bělohorská 130
160 00 Praha 6
Tel.: 777 221 075
Fax: 220 960 592
pensionen@pragpension.cz
www.praghotels.cz oder
www.pragpension.cz
This less expensive hotel is situated right behind Prague Castle.

Campsites

An especially charming institution is the Autocamp Skalice on the Vltava reservoir Slapy, about 35 km south of Prague. One can either pitch tents or camp in little wooden huts for four persons right on the bank of the reservoir. Keen swimmers can find good opportunities for swimming and watersports. Surfboards can be rented on an hourly basis at the wooden gangplank. This beautiful landscape is a paradise for walkers and bicyclists.

Autocamp Skalice
Slapy 2254
252 08 Slapy
Tel./Fax: 257 750 402
autokemp@seznam.cz
www.chatky.cz

Intercamp Kotva Praha
U ledáren 55
147 00 Praha 4
Tel.: 244 466 085
www.kotvacamp.cz

Caravan Camping
Císařská louka 162
150 00 Praha 5
Tel.: 257 317 555
www.caravancamping.cz

Clubs, Discos and Jazz

Rock Café
Národní 20
110 00 Praha 1
Tel.: 224 933 947
www.rockcafe.cz
Live music ranging from punk to ethno music.

Lucerna Music Bar
Vodičkova 36
110 00 Praha 1
Tel.: 224 217 108
www.musicbar.cz
Jazz concerts.

Malostranská beseda
Malostranské náměstí 21
118 00 Praha 1
Tel.: 257 532 092
www.mb.muzikus.cz
Rock- and jazz concerts.

Blues Sklep
Liliová 10
110 00 Praha 1
Tel.: 221 732 066
www.joesgarage.cz/bluessklep
Live international music especially blues, folk and jazz.

AghARTa
Železná 16
110 00 Praha 1
Tel.: 222 211 275
www.agharta.cz
Live jazz music daily.

Reduta
Národní 20
110 00 Praha 1
Tel.: 224 933 487
www.redutajazzclub.cz
Bill Clinton played saxophone here.

Metropolitan Jazz Club
Jungmannova 14
110 00 Praha 1
Tel.: 224 947 777
www.metropolitanmusic.cz
Traditional jazz, mainly Czech bands.

Klub Lávka
Novotného lávka 1
110 00 Praha 1
Tel.: 222 222 156
www.lavka.cz
Discotheque with seven bars, go-go dancers and an open-air dance floor at the riverside.

Roxy
Dlouhá 33
110 00 Praha 1
Tel.: 224 826 296
www.roxy.cz
Experimental music. Underground, international bands.

Radost FX
Bělehradská 120
120 00 Praha 2
Tel.: 224 254 776
www.radostfx.cz
Techno and house music.

Palác Akropolis
Kubelíkova 27
130 00 Praha 3
Tel.: 296 330 911
Fax: 296 330 912
www.palacakropolis.cz
Latin, reggae, hip-hop, funk, house music.

Karlovy lázně
Smetanovo nábřeží 198
110 00 Praha 1
Tel.: 222 220 502
www.karlovylazne.cz
Disco, largest music club and dance floor in Prague.

Meloun
Michalská 12
110 00 Praha 1
Tel.: 224 230 126
www.meloun.cz
Karaoke bar and disco.

Music Club N 11
Národní 11
110 00 Praha 1
Tel.: 222 075 109
www.n11.cz
Rock, pop, blues, funk, disco, concerts with national and international bands.

Club Nebe
Křemencova 10
110 00 Praha 1
Tel.: 224 930 343
Fax: 224 930 344
Hotspot; house, groove, punk.

Duplex
Václavské náměstí 21
113 60 Praha 1
Tel.: 224 232 319
www.duplexduplex.cz
Multi-storeyed disco, techno, r'n'b, funk.

Mecca
U Průhonu 3
170 00 Praha 7
Tel.: 283 870 522
Fax: 283 871 521
www.mecca.cz
House music.

U Staré paní
Michalská 9
110 00 Praha 1
Tel.: 603 551 680
www.jazzlounge.cz
Jazz music.

Internet-Cafés

Káva Káva Káva
Národní 416/37
110 00 Praha 1
Tel.: 224 228 862
www.kava-coffee.cz

Spika
Dlážděná 4
110 00 Praha 1
Tel.: 224 211 521
spika@spika.cz
www.netcafe.spika.cz

Tigger Coffee Bar
U Železné lávky 6
118 00 Praha 1
Tel.: 608 113 112
www.tigger.aktualne.cz

Club Net Café
Americká 39
120 00 Praha 2
Tel.: 602 466 293
www.wumex.cz/netcafe

Coffee Houses and Cafés

Kavárna Slavia
Smetanovo nábřeží 2
110 00 Praha 1
Tel.: 224 218 493

Traditional "theatre café" for visitors to the neighbouring National Theatre. Several Czech intellectuals frequented the Slavia during the first half of the 20ᵗʰ century – hence the name – even Guillame Apollinaire and Rainer Maria Rilke did this place the honours. This spacious café with its generous windows opens the view to the panorama and the bustle of the city.

Café Savoy
Vítězná 5
150 00 Praha 5
Tel.: 257 311 562
www.ambi.cz

Wouldn't anyone rejoice at the resurrection of an old Prague coffee house that was rumoured to be dead!

Grand Hotel Evropa
Václavské náměstí 25
110 00 Praha 1
Tel.: 224 215 387

Most beautiful art nouveau café in Prague. Occasional piano music.

Grand Café Orient
Ovocný trh 19
110 00 Praha 1
Tel.: 224 224 240
www.grandcafeorient.cz

The world's only cubist coffee house.

Café Chef
Ondříčkova 20
130 00 Praha 3
Tel.: 222 710 049

Cozy atmosphere, tasteful furnishings, exquisite homemade cakes and sweets.

Café Louvre
Národní 20
110 00 Praha 1
Tel.: 224 930 949
Traditional coffeehouse with several billiard tables. Kafka and Rilke frequented the "Louvre".

Café de Paris
Hotel Paříž
U Obecního domu 1
110 00 Praha 1
Tel.: 222 195 816
This French art nouveau café belongs to the hotel with the same name and demonstrates apart from a splendid stylish décor also a menu for refined taste combined with noble charges.

Franz Kafka Café
Široká 12
110 00 Praha 1
Tel.: 222 318 945
Cozy relatively new café in the Old Town. Retro furnishings.

Kavárna Vyšehrad inside the Municipal House
náměstí Republiky 5
110 00 Praha 1
Tel.: 222 002 763
Elegant art nouveau café, table in front of the café at the Republic Square in summer.

Chez Marcel
Haštalská 12
110 00 Praha 1
Tel.: 222 315 676
A French bistro on the Vltava, nice atmosphere, revolving football tables.

Restaurants and Pubs

Provided one was served courteously, it is usual to leave about 10% of the bill as a tip in Czech restaurants. VAT is included in the prices on the menu. A cover charge is not common in Prague but some tourist retaurants put it on the bill.

A very informative website in Czech and English gives extensive information about the Prague restaurant and pub scene: www.czechdineout.com informs about prices, special offers, addresses, telephone numbers, opening hours etc. of most of the pubs, restaurants, wine bars, cafés, bars, bistros, pizzerias etc. in Prague.

Czech Cuisine

U Modré kachničky
Michalská 16
110 00 Praha 1
Tel.: 224 213 418

U Zlaté hrušky
Nový svět 3
118 00 Praha 1
Tel.: 220 514 778

Pálffyho Palác
Valdštejnská 14
118 01 Praha 1
Tel.: 257 530 522

Baráčnická rychta
Tržiště 23
118 00 Praha 1

Novoměstský pivovar
Vodičkova 20
110 00 Praha 1
Tel.: 222 232 448

U Fleků
Křemencova 11
110 00 Praha 1
Tel.: 224 934 019-20

U Malířů
Maltézské náměstí 11
118 00 Praha 1
Tel.: 257 530 000

Pivnice U Sv. Tomáše
Letenská 12
118 00 Praha 1
Tel.: 257 531 835

Hostinec U Kalicha
Na Bojišti 12–14
120 00 Praha 2
Tel.: 296 189 600

Klub architektů
Betlémské náměstí 169/5a
110 00 Praha 1
Tel.: 224 401 214

French Cuisine

La Perle de Prague
Rašínovo nábřeží 80
120 00 Praha 2
Tel.: 221 984 160

La Provence
Štupartská 9
110 00 Praha 1
Tel.: 257 535 050

Italian Cuisine

Pizzeria Kmotra
V jirchářích 12
110 00 Praha 1
Tel.: 224 915 809

Ambiente
Mánesova 59
120 00 Praha 2
Tel.: 222 727 851, 222 727 858
www.ambi.cz

Ambiente
Celetná 11
110 00 Praha 1
Tel.: 224 230 244
www.ambi.cz

Ostroff
Střelecký ostrov 336
110 00 Praha 1
Tel.: 224 934 028
www.ostroff.cz

Asian Cuisine

Saté
Pohořelec 3
118 00 Praha 1
Tel.: 220 514 552

Taj Mahal
Škrétova 10
120 00 Praha 2
Tel.: 224 225 566

Orange Moon
Rámová 5
110 00 Praha 1
Tel.: 222 325 119

International Cuisine

Reykjavik
Karlova 20
110 00 Praha 1
Tel.: 222 221 218

Pasha
U Lužického semináře 23
118 00 Praha 1
Tel.: 257 532 434

Cantina
Újezd 38
118 00 Praha 1
Tel.: 257 317 173

Nebozízek
Petřínské sady 411
118 00 Praha 1
Tel.: 257 315 329

Parnas
Smetanovo nábřeží 2
110 00 Praha 1
Tel.: 224 218 521

Vegetarian Cuisine

Country Life
Melantrichova 15
110 00 Praha 1
Tel.: 224 213 366

Lotos
Platnéřská 13
110 00 Praha 1
Tel.: 222 322 390

Museums and Galleries

Jewish Museum
[Židovské muzeum]

U Staré školy 1
110 00 Praha 1
Tel.: 224 819 456
Fax: 224 819 458
office@jewishmuseum.cz
www.jewishmuseum.cz
Opening hours:
Nov.–Mar. 9 a.m.–4.30 p.m.
Apr.–Oct. 9 a.m.–6 p.m.

This museum founded in 1906 documents at length the tradition of Jewish life in Bohemia. All institutions of the Jewish Museum are open daily, except Saturdays and Jewish holidays.

Old Ceremonial Hall
[Obřadní síň – budova
pražského Pohřebního bratrstva]
U Starého hřbitova 3a
110 00 Praha 1
zmp@ecn.cz
www.jewishmuseum.cz

An exhibition demonstrates the work of the Funeral Brethren and informs about Jewish funeral rites.

"Klausen" Synagogue
[Klausová synagoga]
U Starého hřbitova
110 00 Praha 1
Tel.: 222 310 302
Fax: 222 317 181
zmp@ecn.cz
www.jewishmuseum.cz

Jewish traditions, like religious celebrations and everyday customs, for example kosher cooking, are introduced here.

Maisel Synagogue
[Maiselova synagoga]
Maiselova 8–10
110 00 Praha 1
Tel.: 224 810 099-131
Fax: 222 310 681
zmp@ecn.cz
www.jewishmuseum.cz

A part of the collection "Silver from Bohemian synagogues" and an exhibition about the history of Jews in Bohemia is on display here.

Pinkas Synagogue
[Pinkasova synagoga]
Široká 3
110 00 Praha 1
Tel.: 222 326 660
zmp@ecn.cz
www.jewishmuseum.cz

There is a memorial for the victims of the holocaust inside the synagogue. There is also an exhibition of paintings by children from the concentration camp Theresienstadt [Terezín].

Robert Guttmann Gallery
[Galerie Roberta Guttmanna]
U Staré školy 3
110 00 Praha 1
www.jewishmuseum.cz

This Jewish Museum Gallery is named after a painter of the First Republic from the Bohemian Forest. Robert Guttmann, who lived in Prague since 1895, sympathised with the, at that times, new Zionist movement. He died in 1942 in the ghetto in Łódź.

Spanish Synagogue
[Španělská synagoga]
Dušní 12/Vězeňská 1
110 01 Praha 1
Tel.: 224 819 464
www.jewishmuseum.cz
www.bejt-praha.cz

An exhibition reports on the history of Jews in Bohemia from the Jewish emancipation in the 19th century until present times.

Prague City Gallery
[Galerie hlavního města Prahy]

Staroměstská Town Hall
[Staroměstská radnice]
Staroměstské náměstí 1
110 00 Praha 1
Tel.: 224 482 751
www.citygalleryprague.cz
Opening hours:
Daily except Mondays
Apr.–Oct. 9 a.m.–6 p.m.
Nov.–Mar.10 a.m.–5 p.m.

The museum is located on the second floor.
Changing exhibitions.

House "At the Golden Ring"
[Dům U Zlatého prstenu]
Týnská 6
110 00 Praha 1
Tel.: 224 827 022-4
www.citygalleryprague.cz
Opening hours:
Daily 10 a.m.–6 p.m. except Mondays.

Czech art of the 20th century is displayed on three floors.

Bílek-Villa
[Bílkova vila]
Mickiewiczova 1
160 00 Praha 6
Tel.: 224 322 021
www.citygalleryprague.cz
Opening hours:
Saturday and Sunday. 10 a.m.–5 p.m.

The works of the sculptor František Bílek can be seen in his home.

Statues in front of the Bílek-Villa.

Municipal Library
[Městská knihovna]
Mariánské náměstí 1
110 00 Praha 1
Tel.: 222 310 489, 222 313 357
www.citygalleryprague.cz
Opening hours:
Daily 10 a.m.– 6 p.m. except Mondays.

The museum is situated on the second floor. Exhibitions change.

House "At the Stone Bell"
[Dům U Kamenného zvonu]
Staroměstské náměstí 13
110 00 Praha 1
Tel.: 222 327 677
www.citygalleryprague.cz
Opening hours:
Daily 10 a.m.–6 p.m. except Mondays.

Exhibitions change.

Troja Chateau
[Trojský zámek]
U Trojského zámku 1
170 00 Praha 7
Tel.: 283 851 626
www.citygalleryprague.cz
Opening hours:
Daily 10 a.m.–6 p.m. except Mondays, in the wintermonths only Sat.and Sun. 10 a.m.–5 p.m.

This museum houses an exhibition of Czech painting of the 19th century and Czech sculpture from the years 1900 to 1970.

Prague City Museum
[Muzeum hlavního města Prahy]

Main building
[Hlavní budova]
Na Poříčí 52
186 00 Praha 8
Tel.: 224 816 772-3
Fax: 224 214 306
www.muzeumprahy.cz
Opening hours:
Daily 9 a.m.–6 p.m. except Mondays.

Prague's development since the primeval times until the year 1620 is shown in this museum.

Müller-Villa (also Loos-Villa)
[Müllerova vila (Loosova vila)]
Nad Hradním vodojemem 14
160 00 Praha 6
Tel.: 224 312 012
vila.muller@muzeumprahy.cz
www.muzeumprahy.cz
Opening hours:
Apr.–Oct. Tues., Thurs., Sat.
and Sun. 9 a.m.–6 p.m.
Nov.–Mar. Tues., Thurs., Sat.
and Sun. 10 a.m.–5 p.m.

This villa built by the Austrian architect Adolf Loos can only be viewed by prior reservation at the above-mentioned telephone number or e-mail address.

Výtoň
Rašínovo nábřeží 412
120 00 Praha 2
Tel.: 224 919 833
www.muzeumprahy.cz
Opening hours:
Daily 10 a.m.–5 p.m. except Mondays, first Thursday of the month until 8 p.m.

Documents about the history of rafting and steam navigation on the Vltava are displayed in this museum.

National Gallery
[Národní galerie]

Czech Cubism Museum (House of the Black Madonna)
[Muzeum českého kubismu
(Dům U Černé Matky Boží)]

Ovocný trh 19
110 01 Praha 1
Tel.: 224 211 746
www.ngprague.cz
Opening hours:
Daily 10 a.m.–6 p.m.
except Mondays.

An interesting collection of objects of Czech cubism is exhibited in Europe's first cubist building.

Kinsky Palace
[Palác Kinských]
Staroměstské náměstí 12
110 00 Praha 1
Tel.: 224 810 758 / Fax: 222 329 331
www.ngprague.cz
Opening hours:
Daily 10 a.m.–6 p.m. except Mondays.

The long-term exhibition "Landscape in Czech Art (17th–20th century)" can be viewed here.

St Agnes Convent
[Klášter sv. Anežky České]
U Milosrdných 17/Anežská 1
110 00 Praha 1
Tel.: 224 810 628 / Fax: 221 879 217
www.ngprague.cz
Opening hours:
Daily 10 a.m.–6 p.m. except Mondays.

In the former convent a collection of medieval arts and crafts is exhibited.

National Gallery – Modern and Contemporary Art
[Veletržní palác – Sbírka moderního
a současného umění]
Dukelských hrdinů 47
170 00 Praha 7
Tel.: 224 301 024 / Fax: 224 301 056
www.ngprague.cz
Opening hours:
Daily 10 a.m.–6 p.m. except Mondays.

Works of international artists (19th and 20th century) are displayed on several floors in this functionalistic building.

St George's Convent
[Klášter sv. Jiří]
Jiřské náměstí 33
119 04 Praha 1
Tel.: 257 320 536 / Fax: 257 532 234
www.ngprague.cz
Opening hours:
Daily 10 a.m.–6 p.m. except Mondays.

Bohemian art of mannerism and Baroque (for example, works of Karel Škréta, Peter Brandl, Adrian de Vries etc.).

Zbraslav Castle
[Zámek Zbraslav]
Bartoňova 2
156 00 Praha 5
Tel.: 257 921 638-9
Fax: 257 920 482
www.ngprague.cz
Opening hours:
Daily 10 a.m.–6 p.m. except Mondays.

There is a museum of Asian art in this castle. Apart from Chinese and Japanese works, there are also Indian and Tibetan pieces as well as exhibits from the Near East.

Sternberg-Palace
[Šternberský palác]
Hradčanské náměstí 15
119 04 Praha 1
Tel.: 220 514 637-7
Fax: 220 513 180
www.ngprague.cz
Opening hours:
Daily 10 a.m.–6 p.m. except Mondays.

Extensive collection of European art from classical antiquity to Baroque; besides noted Dutch masters, also the works of Tiepolo, El Greco, Goya, Dürer, Holbein and Lukas Cranach.

National Museum
[Národní muzeum]

Antonín Dvořák-Museum
[Muzeum Antonína Dvořáka]
Ke Karlovu 20
120 00 Praha 2
Tel.: 224 923 363
Fax: 224 923 363
www.nm.cz
Opening hours:
Daily ca 10 a.m.–5 p.m. except Mondays.

This museum in the Baroque summer-palace "Vila Amerika" houses the famous Czech composer Antonín Dvořák's desk and several of his music scores.

Bedřich Smetana-Museum
[Muzeum Bedřicha Smetany]
Novotného lávka 1
110 00 Praha 1
Tel.: 222 220 082
Fax: 222 220 082
www.nm.cz
Opening hours:
Daily 10 a.m.–12 a.m. and 12.30–5 p.m. except Tuesdays.

This museum exhibits original manuscripts and letters of the composer and also Smetana's piano as well as several costumes from his operas.

Lapidarium ▲
Výstaviště 422
170 05 Praha 7
Tel.: 233 375 636
Fax: 224 226 488
www.nm.cz
Opening hours:
Tues.–Fri. 12 a.m.–6 p.m. und Sat. and Sun. 10 a.m.–6 p.m.

Sculptures from all epochs including the original sculptures from the Charles Bridge are exhibited in this building constructed in 1891.

National Museum
[Národní muzeum]
Václavské náměstí 68
115 79 Praha 1
Tel.: 224 497 111
Fax: 222 246 047
www.nm.cz
Opening hours:
May–Sept. 10 a.m.–6 p.m.
Oct.–Apr. 9 a.m.–5 p.m.

This impressive building enthroned at the upper end of Wenceslas Square houses extensive collections relating to natural sciences and archeology. The museum was established in 1818 and is not only the largest but also the oldest Czech museum.

Palais Lobkowicz
[Lobkovický palác]
Jiřská 3
119 00 Praha 1
Tel.: 257 535 121
Fax: 233 354 467
www.nm.cz
www.hrad.cz
Opening hours:
Daily 9 a.m.–5 p.m. except Mondays.

An exhibition of national history is set up in this spacious palace.

Ethnological Museum
[Náprstkovo muzeum]
Betlémské náměstí 1
110 00 Praha 1
Tel.: 222 221 416
www.aconet.cz/npm
Opening hours:

Daily 10 a.m.–6 p.m. except Mondays.
Various long-term exhibitions offer an interesting insight into the cultures of the native inhabitants of America, Asia, Australia and Oceania.

Other Museums

Bertramka
Mozartova 169
150 00 Praha 5
Tel.: 257 317 465 / Fax: 257 316 753
www.bertramka.cz
Opening hours:
Apr.–Oct. 9.30 a.m.–6 p.m.
Nov.–Mar. 9.30 a.m.–4 p.m.

Most important Mozart memorial in Prague.

Alfons Mucha-Museum
[Muzeum Alfonse Muchy]
Panská 7
110 00 Praha 1
Tel.: 224 216 415
info@mucha.cz
www.mucha.cz
Opening hours:
Jan. and Feb. 10 a.m.–4 p.m.
Mar.–Dec. 10 a.m.–6 p.m.

The almost one hundred exhibits offer a good insight int the versatile work of the famous art nouveau artist Alfons Mucha (1860–1939).

Army Museum
[Armádní muzeum –
Historický ústav Armády ČR]
U Památníku 2
130 05 Praha 3
Tel.: 973 204 924
Fax: 973 541 308
www.militarymuseum.cz
Opening hours:
Daily 10 a.m.–6 p.m. except Mondays.

A permanent exhibition of the history of the Czechoslovakian Army and its role (especially in the years 1914–1918 and 1939–1945) can be viewed here.

Franz Kafka Exhibition
[Expozice Franze Kafky]
náměstí Franze Kafky 5
110 00 Praha 1
Tel.: 222 321 675
Opening hours:
Tues.–Fri. 10 a.m.–6 p.m.
Sat. 10 a.m.–5 p.m.

A small exhibition documents briefly the life and works of Franz Kafka.

Prague Castle Gallery of Paintings
[Obrazárna Pražského hradu]
Prague Castle – Second Courtyard
119 08 Praha 1
Tel.: 224 373 531 / Fax: 224 310 896
www.hrad.cz
Opening hours:
Daily 10 a.m.–6 p.m.

The remnants of the historical Rudolphine Art Collection with works of Tintoretto, Tizian und Rubens are shown in this museum.

Kampa Museum
[Muzeum Kampa (Sovovy mlýny)]
U Sovových mlýnů 2
118 00 Praha 1
Tel.: 257 286 147
Fax: 257 286 113
www.museumkampa.cz
Opening hours:
Daily 10 a.m.–6 p.m.

Works of 20th century Czech artists are on display in this recently renovated museum.

Museum of Decorative Arts
[Uměleckoprůmyslové muzeum]
17. listopadu 2
110 00 Praha 1
Tel.: 251 093 111
Fax: 224 811 666
www.upm.cz
Opening hours:
Daily 10 a.m.–6 p.m. except Mondays.

The world's largest glass collection shows almost a total of over 16,000 exhibits made of glass, porcelain or ceramic. There's also a section with clocks, measuring devices and cubist furniture.

Police Museum
[Muzeum Policie ČR]
Ke Karlovu 1
120 00 Praha 2
Tel.: 224 923 619
Fax: 261 441 091
www.mvcr.cz/2003/muzeum_info.html
Opening hours:

Daily 10 a.m.–5 p.m. except Mondays. The exhibition shows apart from arms, a reconstructed scene of crime, narrates famous criminal cases and reports facts worth knowing from the history of the Czech police.

Prague Loretto Shrine
[Loreta]
Loretánské nám. 7
118 00 Praha 1
Tel.: 220 516 740
Fax: 220 516 740
www.loreta.cz
Opening hours:
Daily 9 a.m.–12.15 p.m. and
1 p.m.–4.30 p.m. except Mondays.

The Loretto Treasure, a collection of religious art objects from the 16th–18th century, is stored in the museum of this Marian place of pilgrimage. The most valuable gem is a monstrance adorned with 6,222 diamonds.

Toy Museum
[Muzeum hraček]
Jiřská 6
119 01 Praha 1
Tel.: 224 372 294
Fax: 224 372 295
www.barbiemuseum.cz
Opening hours:
Daily 9.30 a.m.–5.30 p.m.

This museum houses the second largest toy collection in the world and has exhibits from the times of classical antiquity into the present.

Strahov Picture Gallery
[Strahovská obrazárna]
Strahovské nádvoří 1
118 00 Praha 1
Tel.: 233 107 722
Fax: 233 107 752
www.strahovskyklaster.cz
Opening hours:
Daily 9 a.m.–12 a.m. and 12.30–5 p.m.
except Mondays.

This significant monastery collection consists, besides Gothic paintings – the Strahov Madonna is well-known – also works from Baroque and rococo as well as the 19th century.

National Technical Museum
[Národní technické muzeum]
Kostelní 42
170 78 Praha 7
Tel.: 220 399 111
Fax: 233 371 801
www.ntm.cz
Opening hours:
Daily 9 a.m.–5 p.m. except Mondays.

Various machines from the beginning of the Industrial Revolution into the present are set up in the 6,000 m² museum established in 1941. The Technical Museum however offers more than just automobiles, airplanes and other vehicles: An almost 1 km long model of a coal mine can be viewed beneath the museum building; trails with optical and acoustic signals are laid out here.

Wax Figure Museum
[Muzeum voskových figurín]
Melantrichova 5
112 79 Praha 1
Tel.: 224 229 852
Fax: 224 230 101
www.waxmuseumprague.cz
Opening hours:
Daily 9 a.m.–8 p.m.

One not only stands opposite Czech and international personalities of the 20th and 21st century but also finds a "Grandstand of Dictators of the World".

Cinema and Film

Czech cinematographie has a very good reputation, Czech films (for example *Kolja*) could also prove themselves in the international market. Miloš Forman (*Amadeus*), the director of Czech origin is well-known among cinemagoers. A series of important films were shot in the lanes of Prague in the past years and the role of Barrandov Filmstudios is unforgettable in film history.

One doesn't have to do without cinema in Prague even if one does not understand Czech. Most international films are screened in the original version (with Czech subtitles). Many Czech websites give information of the current cinema programme and news from the world of cinema:

www.Kinoserver.cz
www.biograf.cz
www.novinky.cz/kultura/prehled

Reductions

Seniors

Seniors over 70 years (identity card must be presented) get reductions on public transport tickets and entrance for various cultural institutions.

Students

On presenting the ISIC (*International Student Identity Card*), students can get reductions on tickets for public transport and entrance tickets for museums, cinemas, galleries and theatre. It is often sufficient to show the student card of the respective university.

Prague Card

This tourist pass includes reduced tickets for museums as also cheaper transport tickets. Students can get a *Prague Card* cheaper. The cards are sold in travel agencies or tourist information centres.

Newspaper and Media

At the kiosks in the centre or in big hotels one finds a large variety of daily and weekly national newspapers as well as several magazines. The German language newspaper *Prager Zeitung* (www.pragerzeitung.cz) and the English *Prague Post* (www.praguepost.cz) are published weekly in Prague itself and both have a detailed events programme section.

The international radio station of *Radio Praha* and informative website: www.radio.cz. are also very interesting.

Tourist Season

Prague always has high season. The city is especially crowded between Christmas and the Epiphany, at Easter, Whitsun and Corpus Christi. The main tourist season in Prague is in July, August, September and October. Travellers wishing to experience a quieter city ought to come here in the second half of January – that is when Prague people are amongst themselves.

Events Calendar

Besides tourist information the Prague Information Centre (PIS) offers information about concerts and events on their webpage www.pis.cz.

January
New Year's concert: Various New Year's concerts are organised at different places all day long on 1st January. Especially popular are the concerts of the Prague Philharmonic Orchestra in the Rudolfinum.

Prague Winter: This well known music and theatre festival with international ensembles also takes place in the Rudolfinum.

February
Holiday World: The largest Prague amusement fair with numerous attractions can be visited on the exhibition grounds *Výstaviště* .

March
Matthew-Fair: On the exhibition grounds *Výstaviště* Prague's oldest amusement park enthralls the young and the old with merry-go-rounds and other attractions.

The **Festival of Contemporary Music** offers concerts with top local musicians in the *Obecní dům*.

The **European Film Days** show alternative festival contributions and retrospectives in the cinemas Lucerna und Aero.

April
Mozart Open: This actually smaller series of events with lesser known works of the composer take place in the Villa Bertramka.

The **International Jazz-Festival** in Lucerna is meanwhile a prominent jazz festival with European significance.

May
On the occasion of the classical music festival **Prague Spring** several foreign musicians perform at different venues in Prague from mid-May to mid-June. One ought to book tickets early enough. (www.festival.cz).

At the meanwhile well-established **Prague Book Fair** (exhibition grounds *Výstaviště*) in mid-May, many regional and international publishers introduce their latest publications.

June
Dance Prague, an ambitious presentation of contemporary dance can be admired at *Divadlo Archa*.

July
At the **Folklore Festival** music and dance groups from all over the country perform in various parts of the town but mainly at Wenceslas Square and Old Town Square.

August
A summer highlight in August is the three week long **Verdi-Festival** in the States Opera.

September
Music lovers should not miss the music and theatre festival **Prague Autumn** in the House of Artists Rudolfinum.

October
"Burčák" (new wine) from Moravia is served in many Prague restaurants.

November
German-language theatre companies present contemporary as well as classical plays from Germany, Austria and Switzerland at various venues in Prague at the **Theatre Festival in German Language**.

December
At Old Town Square and also other places in the inner city, there are **Christmas markets** with the usual mulled wine, sausage and handicrafts stands.

The best view of the Prague **New Year's Fireworks** is from the Prague Castle. Whoever enjoys company (and noise) can watch this spectacle together with thousands of people from here and other countries from the Charles Bridge.

Czech Holidays

01.01.	New Year
variable:	Easter Monday
01.05.	Labour Day
08.05.	Day of Liberation from National socialism
05.07.	Cyril and Method
06.07.	Death Anniversary of Jan Hus
28.09.	St Wenceslas (Day of Czech Sovereignity)
28.10.	Foundation of the Republic
17.11.	Struggle for Freedom and Democracy
24.12.	Christmas Eve
25.12.	First Christmas Holiday
26.12.	Second Christmas Holiday (St Stephen)

Ticket Sales

Ticketpro
Klimentská 22
110 00 Praha 1
Tel.: 296 329 999
Fax: 234 704 204
ticket@ticketpro.cz
www.ticketpro.cz

Ticketcentrum
Rytířská 31
110 00 Praha 1
Tel.: 296 329 999

Weather and Climate

The climate in Prague is continental. Due to its geographical situation it can get very hot in summer. Pleasant temperatures reign in May/June and September/October. Winters are relatively mild, ignoring the occasional frost. Whoever wishes to avoid the overcrowded summer months will be delighted with Prague snow in the wintertime, especially as winter is the peak season for concerts and opera.

Through Prague by Taxi

AAA Taxi	233 113 311
Halotaxi	244 114 411
ProfiTaxi	261 314 151

Taxis are really inexpensive in Prague, but some drivers are dishonest and demand very high fares from tourists. It is recommended therefore to ask about the fare before the ride. Hotel taxis and airport taxis are as a rule a bit more expensive. If one calls for a taxi from the above-mentioned taxi companies the probability of being cheated is less. With a bit of luck, the operator might speak English too, but rarely other languages.

Bus, Tram and Metro

The public transport network in Prague is very well-developed. One can buy tickets for bus, metro and tram at the ticket counters as well as at ticket vending machines in the metro stations or at tobacconist's [trafika]. The tickets should be punched

on entering the means of transport or while passing through the respective barrier in the metro station. The three metro lines run from 5 a.m.–12 p.m. (every three to five minutes), buses and trams ply between 4.30 a.m. and 12 p.m., occasionally even round-the-clock. Buses and trams run at intervals of 10 minutes, the intervals are often increased to 40 minutes at night.

Metro and tram plans are available at the important metro stations (for example Muzeum, Můstek, Anděl).

One can also look up streets or lanes through the internet. The website www.mapy.atlas.cz offers a detailed map and information (hotels, museums, restaurants) in the respective area.

Ticketfares

Ticket 20 min
(five stations) without
transfer possibility   14,- Kč
(Nepřestupní jízdenka)
Children   7,- Kč
  Ticket 75 min with
possibility to transfer   20,- Kč
(Přestupní jízdenka)
Children   10,- Kč
  Day ticket   80,- Kč
(Denní jízdenka)
  3-day ticket   220,- Kč
(Třídenní jízdenka)
  Weekly ticket   280,- Kč
(Týdenní jízdenka)
  15-day ticket   320,- Kč
(15-tidenní jízdenka)
  Monthly ticket   560,- Kč
(Měsíční jízdenka)

Further – and always current – information can be found at the website:
www.dp-praha.cz

To Prague Airport

The airport Prague-Ruzyně is situated 20 km northwest of the city centre and is used by numerous international airlines. The drive from the airport into the city centre takes about 30 to 50 min irrespective of the means of transport.
A taxi drive from the airport into the city centre costs 360–400 Kč. There are various buses to the airport. The probably simplest connection is from Prague 6 – Dejvice [Metro station Dejvická (Line A),and further on with the airport bus until the final stop].

Prague Train Stations

Central Station
[Hlavní nádraží]
Wilsonova
120 00 Praha 2
Central connecting station. All the important regional and international connections leave from the Central Station. Next to the ticket counters in the hall, there are also counters for accommodation arrangements, change bureau, travel agents, kiosks and restaurants.
Metro station Hlavní nádraží (Line C).

Masaryk Station
[Masarykovo nádraží]
Hybernská
110 00 Praha 1
All the connecting regional trains in the direction north and east leave from here. The station is situated between the metro stations Náměstí Republiky (Line B) and Hlavní nádraží (Line C).

Holešovice Station
[Nádraží Holešovice]
Partyzánská
170 00 Praha 7
Connecting station. The trains in directions to Vienna, Dresden, Berlin and Hamburg leave from here. In the hall, next to the ticket counter, there are counters for accommodation, change bureau and shops selling travel accessories.
Metrostation Nádraží Holešovice (Line C).

Smíchov Station
[Smíchovské nádraží]
Nádražní
150 00 Praha 5
Connecting station. International trains stop here before going on to the Central Station. One would get on here for Karlštejn.
Metrostation Smíchovské nádraží (Line B).

Prague Bus Stations

ČSAD
Křižíkova 4
180 00 Praha 8
Metro station Florenc (Line B und C)
Tel.: 900 144 444
www.florenc.info

ČSAD
autobusové stanoviště Holešovice
170 00 Praha 7
Tel.: 900 144 444
www.uan.cz

Train Information
840 112 113;
info@cd.cz;
www.cd.cz

Flight Connections
239 007 007;
call.centre@csa.cz;
www.csa.cz

Bus, Train and Flight Connections
www.jizdnirady.cz

Telephone Calls

Most of the call-boxes in the centre function with phone cards [telefonní karty] that can be bought at the post office, at kiosks and at tobacconists [trafika].

Important Telephone Numbers

International Dialling Codes:

Austria	0043
Czech Republic	00420
France	0033
Germany	0049
Great Britain	0044
Italy	0039
Japan	0081
Poland	0048
Russia	007
Spain	0034
Switzerland	0041
USA	001

Ambulance	155
Police-emergency	158
City Police	156
Fire Brigade	150
Doctors (on call)	183
Pharmacies (24-hour)	184
Directory inquiry inland	1180
Directory inquiry foreign	1181
24-hour-breakdown service	1230

Travelling with Children

Arrangements for baby care are rare in hotels and restaurants. Some hotels offer a babysitter-service.

Children are often welcome in restaurants. Children's dishes are sometimes offered on the menu or one can order smaller helpings.

Prague – *A Guide*

Interesting for Children

Horse-drawn carriages
A great, relatively inexpensive amusement for old and young are the horse-drawn carriage-rides through inner town of Prague with the Prague horse cabs. They leave from Old Town Square.

Ship tour, rowboats or pedalos on the Vltava
Boat rentals:
Slovanský ostrov
110 00 Praha 1

Mirror maze on the Petřín Hill
Petřínské sady
118 00 Praha 1
Tel.: 257 315 212

Divadlo minor
Vodičkova 6
110 00 Praha 1
Tel. 222 231 702; 222 231 351
Fax: 221 416 446
www.minor.cz
Puppet theatre.

Divadlo Spejbla a Hurvínka
Dejvická 38
160 00 Praha 6
Tel.: 224 316 784
www.volny.cz/spejblhurvinek
Puppet theatre.

Toy Museum (see under museums)

A ride on the historical tram route N° 91
Get on at the following stops: Výstaviště, Veletržní, Strossmayerovo náměstí, Nábřeží kapitána Jaroše, Čechův most, Malostranská, Malostranské náměstí, Hellichova, Újezd, Národní divadlo, Národní třída, Lazarská, Vodičkova, Václavské náměstí, Jindřišská, Masarykovo nádraží, Náměstí Republiky, Dlouhá třída.

Sparky's Dům hraček
Havířská 2
110 00 Praha 1
Tel.: 224 239 309
info@sparkys.cz
www.sparkys.cz
Prague's biggest toy shop.

Prague Zoo
U Trojského zámku 3
171 00 Praha 7
Tel.: 296 112 111
Fax: 233 556 708
www.zoopraha.cz

Playgrounds
There is a well-maintained playground complex on the Letná, not far from the metronome. The surrounding park offers numerous possibilities for games too.

Interesting Statistics

Total Area	497 m²
Population	1,2 million
Height	177–397 m above sea level
Administration	22 districts, 57 parts of the city
Business	Significant industrial location of the Czech

Republic. Besides machine and motor manufacturing industry, oil refineries, electrical-, clothing-, printing- and chemical industry, tourism is one of the most significant business factors in Prague.

Municipal Lost and Found Office

Ztráty a nálezy
Karoliny Světlé 5
110 00 Praha 1
Tel.: 224 235 085

Goods for personal use may be taken out of the country on an unlimited basis; an export sanction may be required for certain antiques and objects of art.

Customs Office at the Central Station
(see train stations)

Customs Office Airport Ruzyně
Aviatická 12
160 08 Praha 6
Tel.: 220 113 100
Fax: 266 090 997
info1941@cs.mfcr.cz
www.cs.mfcr.cz

Main Customs Office Prague
Plzeňská 139
150 00 Praha 5
Tel.: 257 019 111
Fax: 257 225 215
info1751@cs.mfcr.cz
www.cs.mfcr.cz

Sport

Prague is always represented in the First League with two to four football clubs which is why there is a home game almost every weekend. Besides *Sparta* and *Slavia,* known even outside the Czech Republic, the football club *Viktoria Žižkov* is very popular in Prague.

The national game, quite clearly, is ice hockey. During the various championships the entire nation fevers in anticipation in front of their televisions or in sports bars with their "hockeyist". An informative website for the English-speaking foreigners living in Prague, that also functions as a forum in other parts of life is: www.expats.cz. One can look up current sports information, fitness institutions etc. Anyone looking for a suitable sports partner, be it a tennis trainer, a volleyball team or a trekking comrade could be successful in finding one here.

Cycling

Keen cyclists can push the pedal anywhere, even in Prague. But this city on the Vltava is not a cyclist's paradise. Few bicycle paths, insane car traffic, bumpy cobblestone streets and a rather hilly terrain. No, the bicycle is not a vehicle for this city. To add to it, cyclists are seen as social outsiders in this city of car lovers. No politician would ever imagine going to work on a bicycle here. Where BMW and Mercedes are status symbols, one can't really win points with a wireframe.

Tennis

SK Slavia Praha
Letenské sady 32
170 00 Praha 7
Tel.: 233 374 033

Erpet
Strakonická 4
150 00 Praha 5
Tel.: 257 321 177, 257 321 229
Fax: 257 319 212
www.erpet.cz

Squash

Esquo Squash Centrum Strahov
Vaníčkova 3
160 00 Praha 6
Tel.: 257 210 032

Erpet
Strakonická 4
150 00 Praha 5
Tel.: 257 321 177, 257 321 229
Fax: 257 319 212
www.erpet.cz

Swimming

Swimming Stadium Podolí
Podolská 74
140 00 Praha 4
Tel.: 241 433 952

Fitness Centres

Fitness Centrum Vagon
Národní 25
110 00 Praha 1
Tel.: 221 085 544

Golf

Golf Club Divoká Šárka
Nad lávkou 5
160 00 Praha 6
Tel.: 774 203 728
golf@bluegreen.cz
www.bluegreen.cz

Erpet
Strakonická 4
150 00 Praha 5
Tel.: 257 321 177, 257 321 229
Fax: 257 319 212
www.erpet.cz

Zámek Štiřín
Ringhofferova 711
251 68 Štiřín
pošta Kamenice
Tel./Fax: 255 736 551
www.stirin.cz

This palace that used to be the property of
the industrialist family Ringhoffer is situated about 25 km southeast of Prague. A
golf course has been set up in the palace
park. You can enjoy a game in a quiet surrounding amidst ponds. There is a five-
star-hotel in the palace.

Tips on Money

1 Czech Crown = 100 Hellers
Coins: 50 Heller; 1, 2, 5, 10, 20
            und 50 Crowns.
Banknotes: 50, 100, 200, 500, 1000,
            2000 und 5000 Crowns.

Changing money at banks is
more feasible than at a change
office. One can also simply draw
money from a cash machine but
must then take in account the service charges. Travellers cheques
in Euros or US Dollars are accepted by banks, change offices,
big shops and hotels. Euros and
US Dollars are rarely accepted in
shops.

Many shops, restaurants and hotels as well as car rentals accept
credit cards.

Changing money on the streets
is principally inadvisable.

Shopping

Anyone wishing to go on a
shopping spree in Prague
should look around Wen-
ceslas Square. "In the ditch"
and Paris Street are the best
known shopping miles in
Prague, but there are many
interesting shops in the Celetná too. Bohemian glass is
a popular souvenir from
the Czech Republic, and
jewellery, children's toys,
antiques, spa wafers, the
green "Becherovka", Prague
ham and plum jam.

Bookshops

Every large bookshop in Prague has foreign language books. A comparison of prices is however advisable because there is no standard pricing in the Czech Republic and the bookshops have different prices.

Vitalis Bookshop
U Lužického semináře 19
118 00 Praha 1
Tel.: 257 530 731
info@vitalis-verlag.com

Jan Kanzelsberger
Václavské náměstí 42
110 00 Praha 1
Tel.: 224 217 335
orbis@volny.cz

The Globe
Pštrossova 6
110 00 Praha 1
Tel.: 224 934 203
globe@globebookstore.cz

Palác Neoluxor
Václavské náměstí 41
110 00 Praha 1
Tel.: 221 111 368
info@neoluxor.cz

Kafkovo knihkupectví
Staroměstské náměstí 12
110 00 Praha 1
Tel.: 222 321 454
franz.kafka@cmail.cz

Knihkupectvi U Černé Matky Boží
Celetná 34
110 00 Praha 1
Tel.: 224 222 349
www.neoluxor.cz

Markets

Havelský trh
Havelská
110 00 Praha 1

One of the oldest weekly markets in the city. One can get cheap fruit and vegetables, wooden toys, handicrafts and jewellery (at times a bit expensive).
Metro station Můstek or Staroměstská (Line A)

Holešovická tržnice
Bubenské nábřeží
170 00 Praha 7

One finds industrial products of all sorts, junk and many eateries in this former slaughterhouse.
Metro station Vltavská (Line C)

Old Town Square
Staroměstské náměstí
110 00 Praha 1
The Old Town Square becomes a marketplace twice a year:

All kinds of handicrafts, lovable and superfluous are on offer before Easter and before Christmas. Fried sausages, beer and mulled wine are readily available.
Metro station Staroměstská (Line A)

There are many more markets in big parking lots on the outskirts where – often by Vietnamese traders – consumer goods are offered, including imitated branded clothes, cheap alcohol, garden gnomes, various electronic items etc.

Medical Provisions for Foreigners

There are some international clinics in Prague where one can be treated in one of the common foreign languages. The medicinal standards in the capital are of international standard.The hospital Na Homolce has a department with English-speaking doctors.

Canadian Medical Care
Veleslavínská 1
162 02 Praha 6
Tel.: 235 360 133
Fax: 220 611 935
cmc@cmc.praha.cz
www.cmc.praha.cz

General Health Care-Clinic Prague
Krakovská 8
110 00 Praha 1
Tel.: 222 211 206
Fax: 222 210 179
ghc@ghc.cz
www.ghc.cz

Health Centre Prague
Vodičkova 28–30
110 00 Praha 1
Tel.: 603 433 833
info@doctor-prague.cz
www.doctor-prague.cz

Pharmacies open round-the-clock

Lékárna Nemocnice Na Františku
Palackého 5
110 00 Praha 1
Tel.: 224 946 982

Lékárna U Anděla
Štefánikova 250/6
150 00 Praha 5
Tel.: 257 324 686
Fax: 257 320 194

Post Office and Postal Charges

24-Hour-Post Office
Jindřišská 14
110 00 Praha 1
Tel.: 221 131 111
info@info.cpost.cz
www.cpost.cz

The Prague postboxes are orange and always bear information about the time the box will be emptied next. A letter within the EU is delivered mostly within two to four days, to other foreign countries within 5 to 10 days.
Since one does not always get stamps with the postcards, one ought to plan a trip to the post-office.

Postal Charges

Inland up to 20g	
(Postcard and letter)	7,50 Kč
Inland up to 50g	12,00 Kč
EU up to 20g	
(Postcard and letter)	10,00 Kč
EU up to 50g	20,00 Kč
Overseas up to 10g	
(Postcard and letter)	11,00 Kč
Overseas up to 20g	12,00 Kč
Overseas up to 50g	24,00 Kč

Travelling by Car

In addition to the national vehicle registration and nationality sign (sticker), car drivers need the green international insurance card.

Seatbelts are obligatory and there is zero tolerance which means no drinking and driving; helmets are compulsory for motorcyclists. Within city limits the speed limit is 50 km/h, outside 90 km/h, on motorways 130 km/h.

Trams generally have right of way.

Most of the motorways and four lane expressways charge a toll. The vignette (sticker) is available at the borders, at post offices and at petrol stations. The vignettes are available for 15 days, two months or one year.

If caught speeding or breaking any other rules, one had better not argue with the official lest it turns out to be expensive.

Parking

While parking one has to take care that the lane remains at least 3 m wide.

There is no waiting or parking on bridges as well as 15 m before and after train crossings, tunnels and underpasses. Green lines on the lane edges means no parking. In Prague centre, there are parking lots mainly for residents (parking license areas marked P and with a blue line), unauthorized parking can mean a high penalty. Since the city police puts wheel clamps [botičky] with incredible speed on cars parked wrongly,

one ought to avoid unauthorized parking. If you are nevertheless in such a situation, call the number on the note left on your windscreen and wait (not rarely, more than an hour) until the mobile police troop comes by and removes the wheel clamp after taking in the cash. Here again: arguments can be counterproductive.

Anyone wishing to avoid this should take one of the watched parking lots (for example directly at the Central Station) or one of the more expensive alternatives (in Kotva at *náměstí Republiky* or the Rudolfinum parking).

Car Rental

A valid passport and driver's license must be presented while renting a car.

A Rent Car

Millenium Plaza
V Celnici 10
110 00 Praha 1
Tel.: 224 211 587
Fax: 224 212 032
info@arentcar.cz
www.arentcar.cz

Airport Ruzyně

Airport Buisness Centre
160 00 Praha 6
Tel.: 224 281 053
Fax: 220 561 976

Prague – *A Guide*

AVIS Rent A Car
Praha City Centre
Klimentská 46
110 02 Praha 1
Tel.: 810 777 810
avis@avis.cz
www.avis.cz

HERTZ
Karlovo náměstí 28
120 00 Praha 2
Tel.: 222 231 010
Fax: 222 231 015
CSPRG60@hertz.cz

Airport Ruzyně
Aviatická
Parking C
160 00 Praha 6
Tel.: 233 326 714
Fax: 220 563 472
CSPRG51@hertz.cz

Foreign Language Church Services

In Prague mass is held in the important foreign languages for foreigners. Most services are Catholic, but Protestant, Orthodox, Baptist and Anglican services are also held in some. The Jewish mass is in Hebrew, Czech and English, the rabbis come from conservative, orthodox and reformed congregations.

German

Church of St Martin in the Wall
(Protestant)
Martinská
110 00 Praha 1
Sundays 10.30 a.m.

Church of St Francis of Assisi
(Catholic)
Křižovnické náměstí
110 00 Praha 1
Saturdays 5 p.m.

Church St Nepomuk on the Rock
(Catholic)
Vyšehradská 49
120 00 Praha 2
Sundays 11 a.m.
(except school holidays)

English

Anglican Community U Klimenta
Klimentská 18
110 00 Praha 1
Sundays 11 a.m.

Baptist Brethren
Vinohradská 68
130 00 Praha 3
Sundays 11 a.m.

Church of St Thomas (Catholic)
Josefská 8
118 00 Praha 1
Saturdays 6 p.m. und Sundays 11 a.m.

Church of Our Lady
of Victory (Catholic)
Karmelitská 9
118 00 Praha 1
Sundays 12 a.m.
(frequent changes, Tel.: 257 533 646)

Church of Augsburg Confession
(Protestant)
Čajkovského 8
130 00 Praha 3
Sundays 11 a.m.

French

Church of St Joseph (Catholic)
Josefská
118 00 Praha 1
Sundays 11 a.m.

Church of Our Lady of Victory
(Catholic)
Karmelitská 9
118 00 Praha 1
Sundays 5 p.m.
(frequent changes, Tel.: 257 533 646)

Italian

Church of the Holy Cross (Catholic)
Na Příkopě 16
110 00 Praha 1
Sundays 11.30 a.m.

Church of Our Lady of Victory
(Catholic)
Karmelitská 9
118 00 Praha 1
Sundays 6 p.m.
(frequent changes, Tel.: 257 533 646)

Korean

Church to Jacob's ladder (Protestant)
U školské zahrady 1/1264
170 00 Praha 7
Sundays 11.30 a.m.

Latin

St Ignatius Church (Catholic)
Karlovo náměstí
120 00 Praha 2
Sundays 11 a.m.

Polish

Church of St Aegidius (Catholic)
Husova 8
110 00 Praha 1
Sundays 12 a.m.

Portuguese

St Thomas Church
Josefská 8
118 00 Praha 1
Every first Sunday at 12.15 p.m.
in the St Barbara Chapel

Slovakian

Church of St Ursula (Catholic)
Národní 8
110 00 Praha 1
Sundays 11 a.m.

Church St Michael in Jircháre
(Protestant)
Jirchářích 9
110 00 Praha 1
Sundays 9.30 a.m.

Spanish

Church of Our Lady of Victory
(Catholic)
Karmelitská 9
118 00 Praha 1
Saturdays 5 p.m.
(frequent changes, Tel.: 257 533 646)

St Thomas Church
Josefská 8
118 00 Praha 1
Sundays 12.30 p.m.

Hungarian

Church of the Bohemian Brethren
(Protestant)
Klimentská 18
Third Floor
110 00 Praha 1
Sundays 4 p.m.

St Bartholomeus Church (Catholic)
Bartolomějská 1
110 00 Praha 1
Every first Sunday of the month
at 1 p.m.

Jewish Services

Old-New Synagogue
Červená 2
Praha 1
Weekdays 8 a.m., Saturdays 9 a.m.,
Fridays and Sundays after sunset.

Jubilee Synagogue
Jeruzalémská
110 00 Praha 1
Saturdays 8.45 a.m., Fridays and
Saturdays after sunset.

Spanish Synagogue
Dušní
110 00 Praha 1
Saturday 10 a.m., Fridays and
Saturdays after sunset.

Tours and Excursions of the City

Anyone wishing to gain an overview
or is interested in special themes (for
example, Franz Kafka and Prague,
music in Prague, mysterious Prague
etc.), can take part in one of the numerous city tours. The groups meet
several times a day below the Astronomical Clock of the City Hall at
the Old Town Square; one can join
in for a fee.

More information is available (in
English and German) on the web
site www.walks.cz

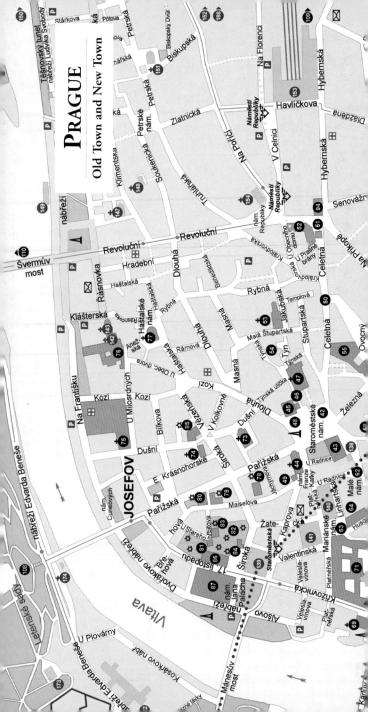

PRAGUE
Old Town and New Town

JOSEFOV

Vltava